D1563483

Design Community College Inc.
PO Box 1153
Topanga CA 90290 USA

info@curedale.com
Designed and illustrated by Robert Curedale

ISBN-10: 0988236257
ISBN-13: 978-0-9882362-5-7

Cover Image: Copyright 2013 Jorg Hackemann , Used under license from Shutterstock.com

Structured Workshops
The author presents workshops online and in person in global locations for executives, engineers, designers, technology professionals and anyone interested in learning and applying these proven innovation methods. For information contact: info@curedale.com

Design Research Methods

150 ways to inform design

Robert Curedale

Dedication

Dedicated to aidan, liam, ashton and clayton

introduction

Design Research has become a required skill for a working designer however few designers were trained in these skills when they studied design. This book contains tools that can be used to inform design as well as ideas about how and when to deploy them effectively so you can be a more successful member of a design team. This book will introduce you to terms used in design research and the value of an evidence-based design approach. These tools can help you to target your design solutions more successfully and discover new ways to differentiate your designs to provide greater value to your clients and target the needs and desires of the people that you are designing for more successfully.

Changes in design practice have meant that there has been a growing divergence between what practising designers were taught at school and the skills that we need to practice design today in an increasingly complex consumer environment. We need to apply new tools that go beyond appearance to navigate the increasing complexity of design practice. Designers need new research practices drawn from social sciences and psychology to successfully uncover user-centered insights in order to create better informed design of products, services, environments and experiences. These tools empower designers to rethink and reinvent the practice of design to discover emerging opportunities to create entirely new designs in rapidly evolving consumer behaviors and global markets.

Did your client ever ask you why you are recommending a particular design concept or direction? Design research supports evidence-based design which is the best way to convince a client that your design concept is based on solid foundations and will be a successful investment.

This book provides quick and practical research techniques that you can use to help base the design on users' needs, desires. You will be introduced to essential research techniques such as affinity diagrams so that you can successfully base your design directions on user-centered evidence to get client buy-in. Design Research is one of the fastest growing areas of design as organizations are trying to target design solutions more accurately and successfully.

The book is intended for business executives who want to create business value and strategic impact through design research, designers of all types, architects and researchers seeking a foundational understanding of design research terms and techniques as well as students.

The methods in this book are an evolution from the traditional approach to design education in a number of ways. The methods help make a designer more effective and efficient when working as part of a multidisciplinary team. They enable a designer to create more successful design by better understanding the outlook of those we are designing for. The methods allow a designer to make informed design decisions that are not only about physical things but also about complex interfaces, systems, services and experiences. In Western economies such as the United States the service sector now employs 90% of the population and organizations that employ designers need to create design that balances the requirements of complex ecosystems of products, environments, services and experiences both physical and virtual.

This is a new approach to design and a different way of seeing the world. These methods can help you work more efficiently and effectively. Four global trends in design require new approaches to designing. These are: the growing focus on people, systems and experiences beyond objects; the growing complexity of the design problems being faced; the trend towards working in cross disciplinary teams; and the growing need to design for distant unfamiliar cultures. These techniques can help you produce design that is innovative and more valuable. This approach is now called Design Thinking. These methods have been tested and successfully applied across disciplines, across cultures, across the globe. They will enable you to design products, systems buildings, interfaces and experiences with confidence that you have created the most informed design solutions for real people that is possible. We believe that this is the largest collection of design methods that is available and with the companion volume two is an indispensable resource for anyone practicing design.

I have kept the descriptions simple to give readers the essential information to adapt, combine and apply the methods in their own way. I hope that you will gradually build a personal toolkit of favored methods that you have tried and found effective. Different design practitioners can select different methods for their toolkit and apply them in different ways. There is no best combination.

contents

8

10

Chapter 1
Thinking Approaches

design thinking

WHAT IS IT?

Design Thinking is a methodology or approach to designing that should help you be more consistently innovative. It involves methods that enable empathy with people, it focuses on people. It is a collaborative methodology that involves iterative prototyping. It involves a series of divergent and convergent phases. It combines analytical and creative thinking approaches. It involves a toolkit of methods that can be applied to different styles of problems by different types of people. Anyone can use Design Thinking. It can be fun.

WHO INVENTED IT?

The origins of new design methods date back to before the 1950s. 1987 Peter Rowe, Professor at the Harvard Graduate School of Design, published "Design Thinking"the first significant usage of the term "Design Thinking" in literature. After 2000 the term became widely used.

CHALLENGES

1. There has been little research to validate claims about Design Thinking by advocates.
2. Some critics of Design Thinking suggest that it is a successful attempt to brand a set of existing concepts and frameworks with a appealing idea.

WHY USE DESIGN THINKING?

Design Thinking is useful when you have:
1. A poorly defined problem.
2. A lack of information.
3. A changing context or environment
4. It should result in consistently innovative solutions.

Design Thinking seeks a balance of design considerations including:
1. Business.
2. Empathy with people.
3. Application of technologies.
4. Environmental consideration.

Design Thinking seeks to balance two modes of thinking:
1. Analytical thinking
2. Creative Thinking

Advocates of Design Thinking believe that the approach results in consistently innovative design solutions oriented towards people.

Design Thinking takes a cross disciplinary team approach. It rejects the idea of a designer being a lone expert artist working in a studio remote from people in favor of an approach where a designer collaborates with a multidisciplinary team. Design Thinking advocates making informed decisions based on evidence gathered from the people and context in place of designers working on a hunch.

WHEN TO USE DESIGN THINKING

Design Thinking is an approach that can be applied throughout the design process:

1. Define intent
2. Know Context
3. Know User
4. Frame insights
5. Explore Concepts
6. Make Plans
7. Deliver Offering

RESOURCES

1. Paper
2. Pens
3. Camera
4. Notebook
5. Post-it-notes
6. Cardboard
7. White board
8. Dry-erase markers

REFERENCES

1. Martin, Roger L. The Opposable Mind: How Successful Leaders Win through Integrative Thinking. Boston, MA: Harvard Business School, 2007.
2. Buchanan, Richard, "Wicked Problems in Design Thinking," Design Issues, vol. 8, no. 2, Spring 1992
3. Cross, Nigel. "Designerly Ways of Knowing." Design Studies 3.4 (1982): 221-27.
4. Brown, Tim, and Katz, Barry. Change by Design: How Design Thinking Transforms Organizations and Inspires Innovation. New York: Harper Business, 2009.
5. Florida, Richard L. The Rise of the Creative Class: and How It is Transforming Work, Leisure, Community and Everyday Life. New York, NY: Basic, 2002 Basic, 2002
6. Jones, John Christopher. Design Methods. New York: John Wiley & Sons, 1970.

design thinking

FOCUS ON PEOPLE:

Design is more about people than it is about things. It is important to stand in those people's shoes, to see through their eyes, to uncover their stories, to share their worlds. Start each design by identifying a problem that real people are experiencing. Use the methods in this book selectively to gain empathy and understanding. and to inform your design. Good process is not a substitute for talented and skilled people on your design team.

GET PHYSICAL

Make simple physical prototypes of your ideas as early as possible. Constantly test your ideas with people. Do not worry about making prototypes beautiful until you are sure that you have a resolved final design. Use the prototypes to guide and improve your design. Do a lot of low cost prototypes to test how Your Ideas physically work. using cardboard, paper, markers, adhesive tape, photocopies, string and popsicle sticks. The idea is to test your idea, not to look like the final product. Expect to change it again. Limit your costs to ten or twenty dollars. Iterate, test and iterate. Do not make the prototype jewelry. It can stand in the way of finding the best design solution. In the minds of some a high fidelity prototype is a finished design solution rather than a tool for improving a design. You should make your idea physical as soon as possible. Be the first to get your hands dirty by making the idea real.

BE CURIOUS

Ask why? Explore and Experiment. Go outside your comfort zone. Do not assume that you know the answer. Look for inspiration in new ways and places. Christopher Columbus and Albert Einstein followed their curiosity to new places.

SEEK TEAM DIVERSITY

A diverse design team will produce more successful design than a team that lacks diversity. Innovation needs a collision of different ideas and approaches. Your team should have different genders, different ages, be from different cultures, different socioeconomic backgrounds and have different outlooks to be most successful. With diversity expect some conflict. Manage conflict productively and the best ideas will float to the surface. Have team members who have lived in different countries and cultures and with global awareness. Cross cultural life experience enables people to be more creative.

TAKE CONSIDERED RISKS

Taking considered risks is helps create differentiated design. Many designers and organizations do not have the flexibility or courage to create innovative, differentiated design solutions so they create products and services that are like existing products and services and must compete on price.
"It takes a lot of courage to release the familiar and seemingly secure, to embrace the new, but there is no real security in what is no longer meaningful. There is more security in the adventurous and exciting, for in movement there is life, and in change, there is power."
Alan Cohen

USE THE TOOLS

To understand the point of view of diverse peoples and cultures a designer needs to connect with those people and their context. The tools in this book are an effective way of seeing the world through the eyes of those people.

LEARN TO SEE AND HEAR

Reach out to understand people. Interpret what you see and hear. Read between the lines. Make new connections between the things you see and hear.

COMBINE ANALYTICAL AND CREATIVE THINKING

Effective collaboration is part of effective design. Designers work like members of an orchestra. We need to work with managers, engineers, salespeople and other professions. Human diversity and life experience contribute to better design solutions.

LOOK FOR BALANCE

Design Thinking seeks a balance of design factors including:
1.   Business.
2.   Empathy with people.
3.   Application OF technology.
4.   Environmental consideration.

TEAM COLLABORATION

Design today is a more complex activity than it was in the past. Business, technology, global cultural issues, environmental considerations, and human considerations all need careful consideration. Design Thinking recognizes the need for designers to be working as members of multidisciplinary multi skilled teams.

The need for creative self expression for designers is important. For an artist the need for creative self expression is a primary need. For a designer this need must be balanced by an awareness and response to the needs of others. Balanced design needs analytical as well as creative thinking. The methods in this book balance a designer's creative thinking with analytical thinking. This balance comes most effectively from a team rather than from an individual. Designers must respond to the needs of the design team, the needs of the business needs of those who employ us to design and the needs of those people that we design for.

design thinking process

DEFINE THE VISION?
What are we looking for?

1. Meet with key stakeholders to set vision
2. Assemble a diverse team
3. Develop intent and vision
4. Explore scenarios of user experience
5. Document user performance requirements
6. Define the group of people you are designing for. What is their gender, age, and income range. Where do they live. What is their culture?
7. Define your scope and constraints
8. Identify a need that you are addressing. Identify a problem that you are solving.
9. Identify opportunities
10. Meet stakeholders

KNOW THE PEOPLE AND CONTEXT
What else is out there?

1. Identify what you know and what you need to know.
2. Document a research plan
3. Benchmark competitive products
4. Create a budgeting and plan.
5. Create tasks and deliverables
6. Explore the context of use
7. Understand the risks
8. Observe and interview individuals, groups, experts.
9. Develop design strategy
10. Undertake qualitative, quantitative, primary and secondary research.
11. Talk to vendors

EXPLORE IDEAS
How is this for starters?

1. Brainstorm
2. Define the most promising ideas
3. Refine the ideas
4. Establish key differentiation of your ideas
5. Investigate existing intellectual property.

PROTOTYPE TEST AND ITERATE
How could we make it better?

1. Make your favored ideas physical.
2. Create low-fidelity prototypes from inexpensive available materials
3. Develop question guides
4. Develop test plan
5. Test prototypes with stakeholders
6. Get feedback from people.
7. Refine the prototypes
8. Test again
9. Build in the feedback
10. Refine again.
11. Continue iteration until design works.
12. Document the process.
13. When you are confident that your idea works make a prototype that looks and works like a production product.

DELIVER
Let's make it. Let's sell it.

1. Create your proposed production design
2. Test and evaluate
3. Review objectives
4. Manufacture your first samples
5. Review first production samples and refine.
6. Launch
7. Obtain user feedback
8. Conduct field studies
9. Define the vision for the next product or service.

critical thinking

WHAT IS IT?

Critical thinking is the discipline of rigorously and skillfully using information, experience, observation and reasoning to guide your decisions, actions and beliefs.

WHO INVENTED IT?

Socrates, Buddhist kalama sutta and Abhidharma.

WHY USE THIS METHOD?

1. More effective decisions
2. More efficient use of time
3. Rational rather than emotion-driven decisions.

WHEN TO USE THIS METHOD

1. Define intent
2. Know Context
3. Know User
4. Frame insights
5. Explore Concepts
6. Make Plans
7. Deliver Offering

HOW TO USE THIS METHOD

Critical thinking skills include:

1. Recognizing and solving problems.
2. Information gathering.
3. Interpreting information.
4. Recognizing relationships.
5. Drawing sound conclusions.
6. Leaning from experience
7. Recognizing assumptions.
8. Self criticism.
9. Self awareness.
10. Reflective thought.
11. Understanding meaning.

REFERENCES

1. Title: Critical Thinking Handbook: K–3rd Grades. A Guide for Remodelling Lesson Plans in Language Arts, Social Studies, and Science. Author: Richard W. Paul, A.J.A. Binker, Daniel Weil. Publisher: Foundation for Critical Thinking. ISBN: 0-944583-05-9
2. Paul, Richard; and Elder, Linda. The Miniature Guide to Critical Thinking Concepts and Tools. Dillon Beach: Foundation for Critical Thinking Press, 2008, p. 4. ISBN 978-0-944583-10-4
3. Ennis, R.H., "Critical Thinking Assessment" in Fasko, Critical Thinking and Reasoning: Current Research, Theory, and Practice (2003). ISBN 978-1-57273-460-9

critical thinking

"Critical thinking is independent thinking for oneself. Many of our beliefs are acquired at an early age, when we have a strong tendency to form beliefs for irrational reasons (because we want to believe, because we are praised or rewarded for believing). Critical thinkers use critical skills and insights to reveal and reject beliefs that are irrational.

In forming new beliefs, critical thinkers do not passively accept the beliefs of others; rather, they try to figure things out for themselves,

They are not limited by accepted ways of doing things. They evaluate both goals and how to achieve them. They do not accept as true, or reject as false, beliefs they do not understand. They are not easily manipulated."

Source: The critical thinking Handbook. Richard W. Paul

AFFECTIVE STRATEGIES

1. Thinking independently
2. Developing insight into egocentricity or sociocentricity
3. Exercising fair-mindedness
4. Exploring thoughts underlying feelings and feelings underlying thoughts
5. Developing intellectual humility and suspending judgment
6. Developing intellectual courage
7. Developing intellectual good faith or integrity
8. Developing intellectual perseverance
9. Developing confidence in reason

Source: The critical thinking Handbook. Richard W. Paul

COGNITIVE STRATEGIES
MACRO-ABILITIES

1. Refining generalizations and avoiding oversimplifications
2. Comparing analogous situations: transferring insights to new contexts
3. Developing one's perspective: creating or exploring beliefs, arguments, or theories
4. Clarifying issues, conclusions, or beliefs
5. Clarifying and analyzing the meanings of words or phrases
6. Developing criteria for evaluation: clarifying values and standards
7. Evaluating the credibility of sources of information
8. Questioning deeply: raising and pursuing root or significant questions
9. Analyzing or evaluating arguments, interpretations, beliefs, or theories
10. Generating or assessing solutions
11. Analyzing or evaluating actions or policies
12. Reading critically: clarifying or critiquing texts
13. Listening critically: the art of silent dialogue
14. Making interdisciplinary connections
15. Practicing Socratic discussion: clarifying and questioning beliefs, theories, or perspectives
16. Reasoning dialogically: comparing perspectives, interpretations, or theories
17. Reasoning dialectically: evaluating perspectives, interpretations, or theories

Source: The critical thinking Handbook. Richard W. Paul

COGNITIVE STRATEGIES
MICRO-ABILITIES

1. Comparing and contrasting ideals with actual practice
2. Thinking precisely about thinking: using critical vocabulary
3. Noting significant similarities and differences
4. Examining or evaluating assumptions
5. Distinguishing relevant from irrelevant facts
6. Making plausible inferences, predictions, or interpretations
7. Giving reasons and evaluating evidence and alleged facts
8. Recognizing contradictions
9. Exploring implications and consequences

Source: The critical thinking Handbook. Richard W. Paul

teaching critical thinking

STRATEGIES

1. Urge students to be reflective
2. Ask such questions as "How do you know", and "Is that a good source of information?"
3. Explore conclusions, explanations, sources of evidence, points of view
4. Discuss problems in the context of realistic situations that students see as significant
5. Ask "Why?"
6. Emphasize seeing things from others' points of view
7. Students do not need to become subject-matter experts before they can start to learn to think critically in a subject
8. Ask students to address questions to which you do not know the answer, or that are controversial. The question should seem significant to them and be interesting
9. Have them work on issues or questions in groups, with each group reporting to the entire class, and each person showing the others what he or she has done.

Source: Robert H. Ennis and Sean F. Ennis.

FRISCO

When appraising a position, whether yours or another's, attend at least to these elements:

1. F for Focus: Identify or be clear about the main point, that is, the conclusion
2. R for Reasons: Identify and evaluate the reasons
3. I for Inference: Consider whether the reasons establish the conclusion, given the alternatives
4. S for Situation: Pay attention to the situation
5. C for Clarity: Make sure that the meanings are clear
6. O for Overview: Review your entire appraisal as a unit

ABILITIES

Critical thinkers:

Care that their beliefs be true and that their decisions be justified;

- Seek alternative hypotheses, explanations, conclusions, plans, sources, etc.; and be open to them
- Consider seriously other points of view than their own
- Try to be well informed
- Endorse a position to the extent that, but only to the extent that, it is justified by the information that is available
- Use their critical thinking abilities

Care to understand and present a position honestly and clearly, theirs as well as others'; including to

- Discover and listen to others' view and reasons
- Be clear about the intended meaning of what is said, written, or otherwise communicated, seeking as much precision as the situation requires
- Determine, and maintain focus on, the conclusion or question
- Seek and offer reasons
- Take into account the total situation
- Be reflectively aware of their own basic beliefs

Care about every person. Caring critical thinkers

- Avoid intimidating or confusing others with their critical thinking prowess, taking into account others' feelings and level of understanding
- Are concerned about others' welfare

Source: Robert H. Ennis and Sean F. Ennis.

REFERENCES

1. Sobocan, Jan & Groarke, Leo   (Eds.), (2009), Critical thinking education and assessment: Can higher order thinking be tested? London, Ontario: Althouse Press.
2. Possin, Kevin (2008). A guide to critical thinking assessment.
3. CRITICAL THINKING Robert H. Ennis1996, Upper Saddle River, NJ: Prentice-Hall ISBN: 0-13-374711-5
4. HOW TO THINK LOGICALLY Gary Seay & Susana Nuccetelli 2008, 592 pgs. Pearson Higher Education ISBN 0321337778

Chapter 4
Know people and context
what is needed?

active listening

WHAT IS IT?
Active listening is a communication method where the listener repeats what they understand to the speaker.

WHO INVENTED IT?
Thomas Gordon coined the term
Carl Rogers 1980

WHY USE THIS METHOD?
1. The ability to listen is an important skill for a designer to demonstrate empathy.

CHALLENGES
1. Listening and hearing or understanding are not the same
2. People give meaning to what they hear.
3. Listening constructs meaning from verbal and non verbal observations.

WHEN TO USE THIS METHOD
1. Know Context
2. Know User

HOW TO USE THIS METHOD
1. The listener observes the speakers body language.
2. This helps the listener understand the speaker's message
3. The listener paraphrases the speakers words to demonstrate understanding of the message.
4. The listener summarizes the issues.

Active listening skills include
1. Posture showing engagement
2. Eye contact
3. Environment that does not distract
4. Appropriate gestures and facial expressions.

REFERENCES
1. Reed, Warren H. (1985). Positive listening: learning to hear what people are really saying. New York: F. Watts. ISBN 0-531-09583-5
2. Atwater, Eastwood (1981). I Hear You. Prentice-Hall. p. 83. ISBN 0-13-450684-7.
3. Novack DH, Dube C, Goldstein MG. Teaching medical interviewing. A basic course on interviewing and the physician-patient relationship. Arch Intern Med 1992;152:1814—2.

activity analysis

WHAT IS IT?
Activity analysis is a method involving observing people in the context of their work.

WHO INVENTED IT?
Thomas Moran

WHY USE THIS METHOD?
1. Observation can reveal ways to make work more effective, efficient and valuable.

CHALLENGES
1. Medium level of cost and time required
2. Analysis may be difficult

WHEN TO USE THIS METHOD
3. Know Context
4. Know User
5. Frame insights

HOW TO USE THIS METHOD
1. Observe work in context
2. Undertake contextual interviews of workers
3. Analyze data
4. Create insights
5. Create Recommendations

RESOURCES
1. Note pad
2. Pens
3. Camera
4. Video camera
5. Digital voice recorder
6. Post-it notes

REFERENCES
1. Garrigou, A., Daniellous, F., Carballeda, G., Ruaud, S. Activity analysis in participatory design and analysis of participatory design activity.1995.

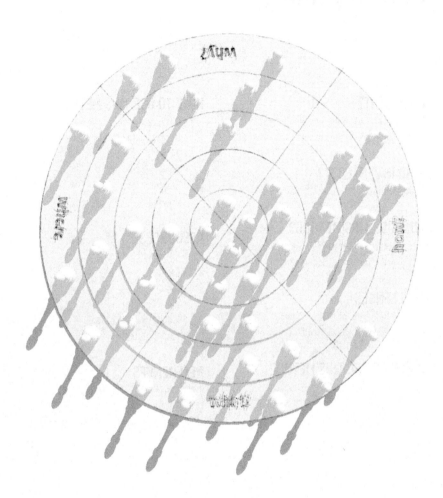

32

actors map

WHAT IS IT?
The Actors Map represents the system of stakeholders and their relationships. It is a view of the service and its context. Stakeholders are organized by their function.

WHY USE THIS METHOD?
1. Understanding relationships is an important aspect of service design.

CHALLENGES
1. This is not a user centered method

WHY USE THIS METHOD?
1. Inexpensive and fast.
2. Connects to existing research tools and methods
3. Makes implicit knowledge explicit
4. Structures complex reality
5. Flexible for use in different contexts.

WHEN TO USE THIS METHOD
1. Know Context
2. Know User
3. Frame insights

SEE ALSO
1. Network map.

REFERENCES
1. (2007) Nicola Morelli, New representation techniques for designing in a systemic perspective, paper presented at Design Inquires, Stockholm.

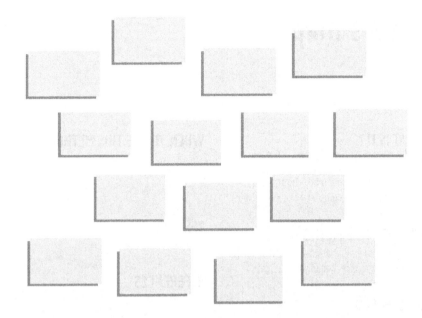

Put individual answers or ideas on post-it-notes Spread post-it-notes or cards on a wall or large table.

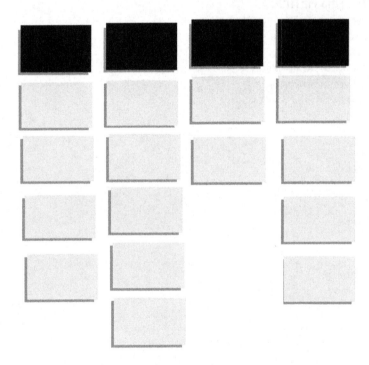

Group similar items and name each group with a different colored card or Post-it-note above the group.

affinity diagram

WHAT IS IT?

Affinity diagrams are a tool for analyzing large amounts of data and discovering relationships which allow a design direction to be established based on the affinities. This method may uncover important hidden relationships.

Affinity diagrams are created through consensus of the design team on how the information should be grouped in logical ways.

WHO INVENTED IT?

Jiro Kawaita, Japan, 1960

WHY USE THIS METHOD?

Traditional design methods are less useful when dealing with complex or chaotic problems with large amounts of data. This method helps to establish relationships of affinities between pieces of information. From these relationships insights and relationships can be determined which are the starting point of design solutions. It is possible using this method to reach consensus faster than many other methods.

RESOURCES

1. White board
2. Large wall spaces or tables
3. Dry-erase markers
4. Sharpies
5. Post-it notes
6. Digital camera

WHEN TO USE THIS METHOD

1. Know Context
2. Know User
3. Frame insights

HOW TO USE THIS METHOD

1. Select your team
2. Place individual opinions or answers to interview questions or design concepts on post-it-notes or cards.
3. Spread post-it-notes or cards on a wall or large table.
4. Group similar items.
5. This can be done silently by your design team moving them around as they each see affinities. Work until your team has consensus.
6. Name each group with a different colored card or Post-it-note above the group.
7. Repeat by grouping groups.
8. Rank the most important groups.
9. Photograph results
10. Analyze affinities and create insights.
11. 5 to 20 participants

REFERENCES

1. Brassard, M. (1989). The Memory Jogger Plus+, pp. 17 – 39. Methuen, MA: Goal/QPC.
2. King, R. (1989). Hoshin Planning, The Developmental Approach, pp. 4-2 – 4-5. Methuen, MA: Goal/QPC.

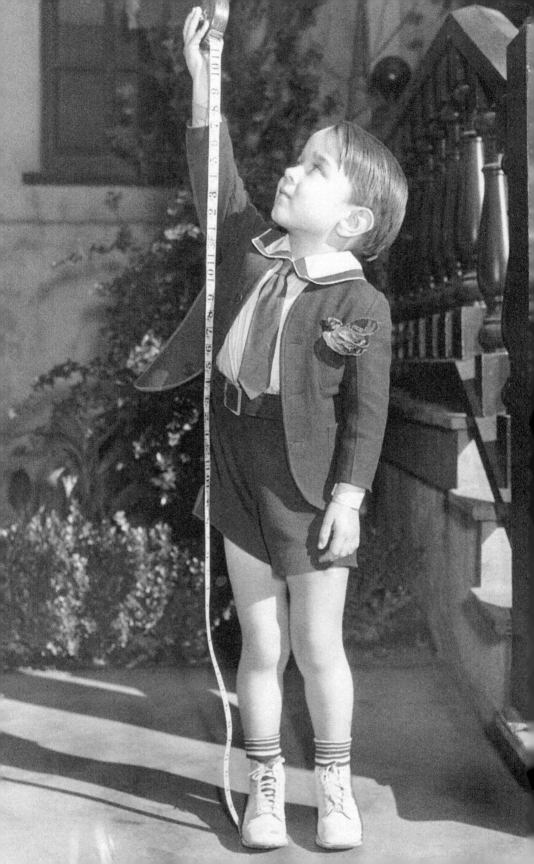

anthropometric analysis

WHAT IS IT?

It is a method of using statistical data about the distribution of body dimensions of people in order to optimize products and spaces.

WHO INVENTED IT?

Louis-Jean-Marie Daubenton 1784

WHY USE THIS METHOD?

Anthropometrics enables designers to properly size items, including system interfaces, to the "fit" the user.

CHALLENGES

1. All people are different but often one design will be used by many people.

RESOURCES

1. Human factors reference data

REFERENCES

1. Pheasant, Stephen (1986). Bodyspace : anthropometry, ergonomics, and design. London; Philadelphia: Taylor & Francis. ISBN 0-85066-352-0.
2. ISO 7250: Basic human body measure-ments for technological design, Interna-tional Organization for Standardization, Humanscale 1-9 by Niels Diffrient, Alvin R. Tilley Published by MIT Press (MA) 1998 026204059X (ISBN13: 9780262040594)

WHEN TO USE THIS METHOD

1. Define intent
2. Know Context
3. Know User
4. Frame insights
5. Explore Concepts

HOW TO USE THIS METHOD

1. Decide who you are designing for
2. Decide which body measurements are relevant
3. Decide whether you are designing for the 'average' or extremes. Consider whether the 5th, 50th, 95th or 100th percentile value may determine the boundaries of the design.
4. Consider Easy reach, A good match between the user and the product, A comfortable and safe posture, Easy and safe operation
5. You may need to add corrections for clothing. Does the user need to wear gloves?
6. You may also need to consider people's eyesight and hearing abilities.

anthropopump

WHAT IS IT?

This method involves the research videotaping one or more participant's activities. The videos are replayed to the participants and they are asked to explain their behavior.

WHO INVENTED IT?

Rick Robinson, John Cain, E- Lab Inc.,

WHY USE THIS METHOD?

1. Used for collecting data before concept and for evaluating prototypes after concept phases of projects,

CHALLENGES

1. Best conducted by someone who has practice observing human interactions in a space.

RESOURCES

1. Video camera
2. Video projector
3. Note pad
4. White board
5. Dry erase markers

WHEN TO USE THIS METHOD

1. Know Context
2. Know User
3. Frame insights

HOW TO USE THIS METHOD

1. People are first captured on video while interacting with products.
2. The participants are then asked to watch the tapes while researchers question them about what they see, how they felt, etc. In effect, research subjects analyses their own actions and experiences.
3. The company invites people who have been captured on video to watch their tapes as researchers pose questions about what's happening.
4. E Lab videotapes and dissects these follow-up sessions, analyzing research subjects analyzing themselves.

Source: [1]

REFERENCES

1. http://www.fastcompany.com/maga-zine/05/october-november-96

autoethnography

WHAT IS IT?

This is research where the researcher studies their own activities and behavior rather than others. May also refer to research of the cultural group that the researcher is part of.

WHO INVENTED IT?

Duncan 1993

WHY USE THIS METHOD?

1. Easy access to self
2. Inexpensive

CHALLENGES

1. Some quantitative researchers consider this method unscientific and unreliable.
2. The study may be too personal
3. May be difficult for the researcher to be objective when studying self.

WHEN TO USE THIS METHOD

4. Know Context
5. Know User
6. Frame insights

RESOURCES

1. Camera
2. Video camera
3. Note pad

HOW TO USE THIS METHOD

1. Be objective
2. Record data while the activity is being undertaken or soon after
3. Analyze and summarize data "
4. Create Reflexive journal summary

REFERENCES

1. Chang, Heewon. (2008). Autoethnography as method. Walnut Creek, CA: Left Coast Press.
2. Duncan, M., Autoethnography: Critical appreciation of an emerging art. International Journal of Qualitative Methods, 3, 4, (2004), Article 3,
3. Ellis, Carolyn. (2004). The Ethnographic I: A methodological novel about autoethnography. Walnut Creek: AltaMira Press.
4. Maréchal, Garance. (2010). Autoethnography. In Albert J. Mills, Gabrielle Durepos & Elden Wiebe (Eds.), Encyclopedia of case study research (Vol. 2, pp. 43–45). Thousand Oaks, CA: Sage Publications.

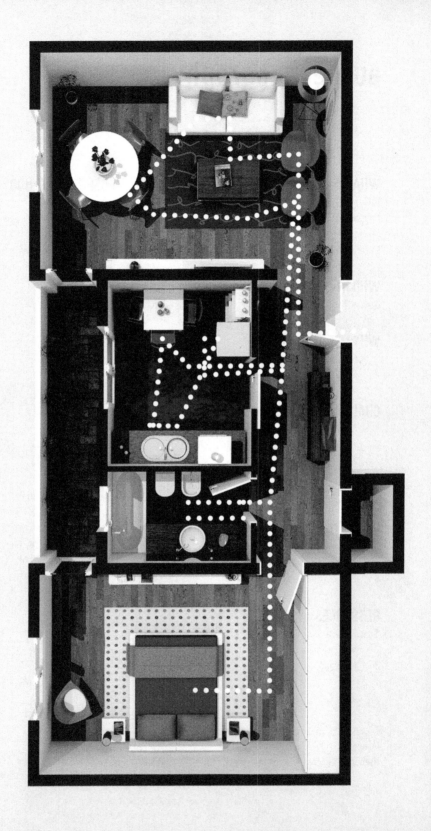

behavioral map

WHAT IS IT?

Behavioral mapping is a method used to record and analyze human activities in a location. This method is used to document what participants are doing and time spent at locations and travelling. Behavioral maps can be created based on a person or a space

WHO INVENTED IT?

Ernest Becker 1962

WHY USE THIS METHOD?

1. This method helps develop an understanding of space layouts, interactions and experiences and behaviors.
2. Helps understand way finding.
3. Helps optimize use of space.
4. A limitation of this method is that motivations remain unknown.
5. Use when you want to develop more efficient or effective use of space in retail environments, exhibits, architecture and interior design.

WHEN TO USE THIS METHOD

1. Define intent
2. Know Context
3. Know User
4. Frame insights
5. Explore Concepts
6.

Image: © Memendesig. | Dreamstime.com

HOW TO USE THIS METHOD

1. Decide who are the users.
2. Ask what is the purpose of the space?
3. Consider what behaviors are meaningful.
4. Consider different personas.
5. Participants can be asked to map their use of a space on a floor plan and can be asked to reveal their motivations.
6. Can use shadowing or video ethnographic techniques.
7. Create behavioral map.
8. Analyze behavioral map.
9. Reorganize space based on insights.

RESOURCES

1. A map of the space.
2. Video camera
3. Digital still camera
4. Notebook
5. Pens

REFERENCES

1. Nickerson 1993: Bnet. Understanding your consumers through behavioral mapping.
2. A Practical Guide to Behavioral Research Tools and Techniques. Fifth Edition Robert Sommer and Barbara Sommer ISBN13: 9780195142099ISBN10: 0195142098

   Aug 2001

CRITERIA	A	B	C	D	E	F	G	H	I
USABILITY	1	2	3	1	4	1	1	2	3
SPEED TO MARKET	2	1	1	2	2	4	2	1	4
BRAND COMPATIBILITY	3	3	4	1	3	0	3	1	2
RETURN ON INVESTMENT	3	3	5	3	0	3	2	1	3
FITS STRATEGY	2	3	1	1	4	1	1	3	3
AESTHETIC APPEAL	1	1	1	4	0	3	1	2	2
DIFFERENTIATION	2	4	0	2	2	4	0	4	4
TOOLING COST	2	2	2	0	1	1	3	3	0
FITS DISTRIBUTION	2	2	1	1	1	2	0	4	3
USES OUR FACTORY	2	2	3	1	2	1	4	0	3
FITS TRENDS	1	3	2	2	1	3	4	3	2
TOTAL	21	26	23	18	20	23	21	24	29

Sample benchmarking matrix for products

benchmarking

WHAT IS IT?
Benchmarking is a method for organizations to compare their products, services or customer experiences with other industry products, services and experiences in order to identify the best practices.

WHO INVENTED IT?
Robert Camp Xerox, 1989
Benchmarking: the search for industry best practices that lead to superior performance.

WHY USE THIS METHOD?
1.   A tool to identify, establish, and achieve standards of excellence.
2.   A structured process of continually searching for the best methods, practices, and processes and either adopting them
3.   The practice of measuring your performance against world-class organizations.

WHEN TO USE THIS METHOD
1.   Define intent
2.   Know Context
3.   Know User
4.   Frame insights

CHALLENGES
1.   Can be expensive
2.   Organizations often think their companies were above the average for the industry when they are not.

HOW TO USE THIS METHOD
1.   Identify what you would like to be bench marked,
2.   Define the process,
3.   Identify potential partners
4.   Identify similar industries and organizations.
5.   Identify organizations that are leaders.
6.   Identify data sources
7.   Identify the products or organizations to be bench marked
8.   Select the benchmarking factors to measure.
9.   Undertake benchmarking
10. Visit the "best practice" companies to identify leading edge practices
11. Analyze the outcomes
12. Target future performance
13. Adjust goal
14. Modify your own product or service to conform with best practices identified in benchmarking process.

RESOURCES
1.   Post-it-notes
2.   Pens
3.   Dry-erase markers
4.   White board
5.   Paper

REFERENCES
1.   Benchmarking for Competitive Advantage. Robert J Boxwell Jr, New York: McGraw-Hill. 1994. pp. 225. ISBN 0-07-006899-2.
2.   Beating the competition: a practical guide to Benchmarking. Washington, DC: Kaiser Associates. 1988. pp. 176. ISBN 978-1-56365-018-5.

blind trials: single blind trial

WHAT IS IT?

He participants do not know if they are in the control or experimental group. The researchers know the test subjects role in the study,

WHO INVENTED IT?

Benjamin Franklin and Antoine Lavoisier, French Academy of Sciences 1784

WHY USE THIS METHOD?

1. Used to eliminate subjective bias by the subjects.

CHALLENGES

1. The tester could intentionally introduce bias

WHEN TO USE THIS METHOD

1. Know Context
2. Know User
3. Frame insights

HOW TO USE THIS METHOD

1. In a single-blind experiment, the participants do not know whether they are "test" subjects or members of an "experimental control" group
2. An example of a single-blind test is the "Pepsi challenge". A moderator has two cups one with Pepsi and one with a competitor's cola and asks a participant to identify the Pepsi. The participant does not know which cup contains the Pepsi.

REFERENCES

1. Friedman, L.M., Furberg, C.D., DeMets, D.L. (2010). Fundamentals of Clinical Trials. New York: Springer, pp. 119-132. ISBN 9781441915856

blind trials: double blind trial

WHAT IS IT?

He participants do not know if they are in the control or experimental group. The researchers do not know which group are subjects and which group is the control group in the study,

WHO INVENTED IT?

Benjamin Franklin and Antoine Lavoisier, French Academy of Sciences 1784

WHY USE THIS METHOD?

1. Used to eliminate subjective bias by both the participants and the research team.

CHALLENGES

1. The tester could intentionally introduce bias

WHEN TO USE THIS METHOD

1. Know Context
2. Know User
3. Frame insights

HOW TO USE THIS METHOD

1. In a single-blind experiment, the participants and the team administering the research do not know whether they are "test" subjects or members of an "experimental control" group

REFERENCES

1. Friedman, L.M., Furberg, C.D., DeMets, D.L. (2010). Fundamentals of Clinical Trials. New York: Springer, pp. 119-132. ISBN 9781441915856

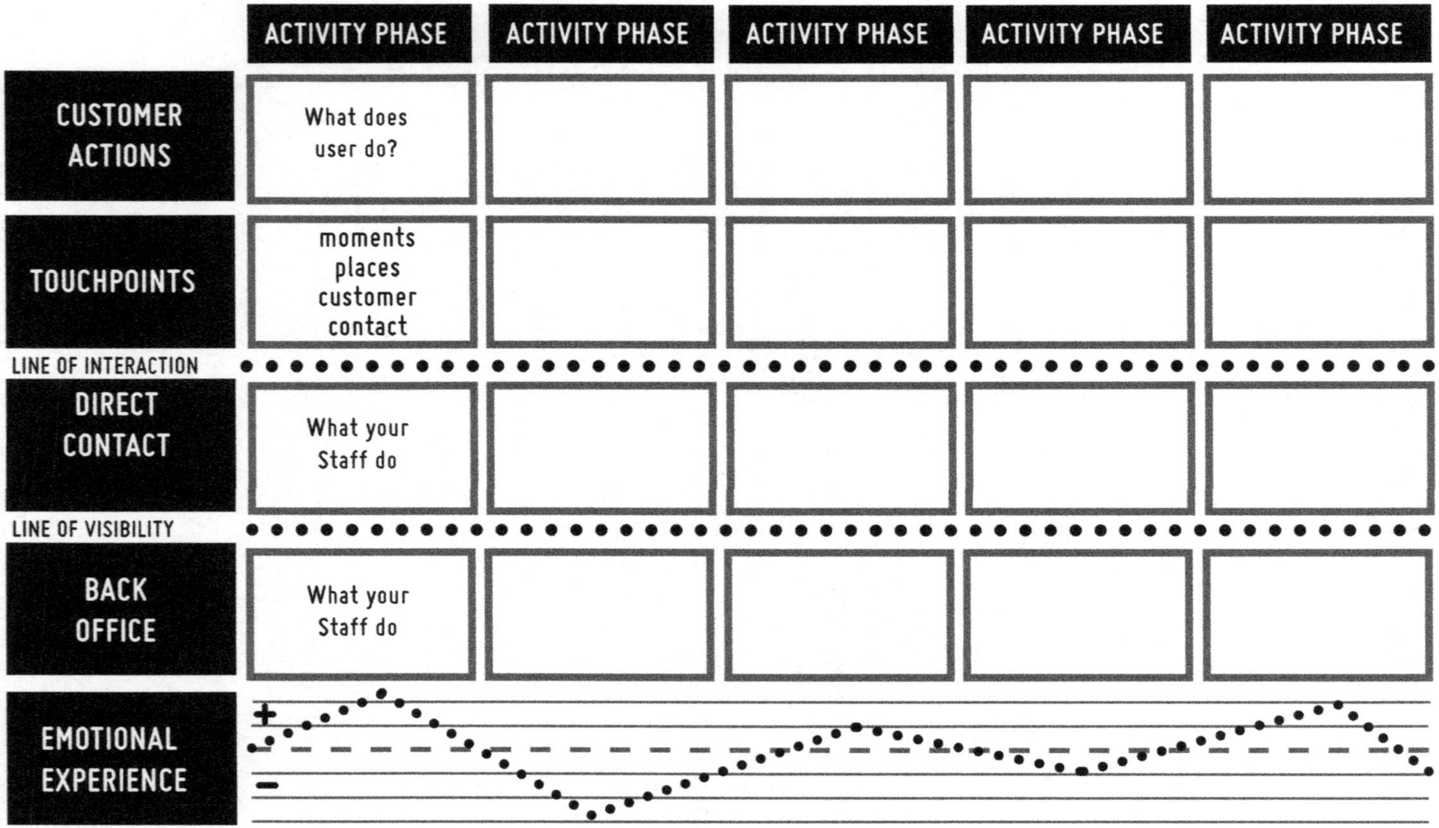
ACTIVITY PHASE
ACTIVITY PHASE
ACTIVITY PHASE
ACTIVITY PHASE
ACTIVITY PHASE
CUSTOMER ACTIONS
What does user do?
TOUCHPOINTS
moments places customer contact
LINE OF INTERACTION
DIRECT CONTACT
What your Staff do
LINE OF VISIBILITY
BACK OFFICE
What your Staff do
EMOTIONAL EXPERIENCE
+
−

blueprint

WHAT IS IT?

A blueprint is a process map often used to describe the delivery of services information is presented as a number of parallel rows of activities. These are sometimes called swim lanes. They may document activities over time such as:

1. Customer Actions
2. Touch points
3. Direct Contact visible to customers
4. Invisible back office actions
5. Support Processes
6. Physical Evidence
7. Emotional Experience for customer.

WHO INVENTED IT?

Lynn Shostack 1983

WHEN TO USE THIS METHOD

1. Know Context
2. Know User
3. Frame insights

WHY TO USE THIS METHOD

1. Can be used for design or improvement of existing services or experiences.
2. Is more tangible than intuition.
3. Makes the process of service development more efficient.
4. A common point of reference for stakeholders for planning and discussion.
5. Tool to assess the impact of change.

HOW TO USE THIS METHOD

1. Define the service or experience to focus on.
2. A blueprint can be created in a brainstorming session with stakeholders.
3. Define the customer demographic.
4. See though the customer's eyes.
5. Define the activities and phases of activity under each heading.
6. Link the contact or customer touchpoints to the needed support functions
7. Use post-it-notes on a white board for initial descriptions and rearrange as necessary drawing lines to show the links.
8. Create the blueprint then refine iteratively.

RESOURCES

1. Paper
2. Pens
3. White board
4. Dry-erase markers
5. Camera
6. Blueprint templates
7. Post-it-notes

REFERENCES

1. (1991) G. Hollins, W. Hollins, Total Design: Managing the design process in the service sector, Trans Atlantic Publications
2. (2004) R. Kalakota, M.Robinson, Services Blueprint: Roadmap for Execution, Addison-Wesley, Boston.

bodystorming

WHAT IS IT?

Bodystorming is method of prototyping experiences. It requires setting up an experience – complete with necessary artifacts and people – and physically "testing" it. A design team play out scenarios based on design concepts that they are developing. The method provides clues about the impact of the context on the user experience.

WHO INVENTED IT?

Buchenau, Fulton 2000

WHY USE THIS METHOD?

1. You are likely to find new possibilities and problems.
2. Generates empathy for users.
3. This method is an experiential design tool. Bodystorming helps design ideation by exploring context.
4. It is fast and inexpensive.
5. It is a form of physical prototyping
6. It is difficult to imagine misuse scenarios

CHALLENGES

1. Some team members may find acting a difficult task.

RESOURCES

1. Empathy tools
2. A large room
3. White board
4. Video camera

WHEN TO USE THIS METHOD

1. Know Context
2. Know User
3. Frame insights
4. Explore Concepts

HOW TO USE THIS METHOD

1. Select team.
2. Define the locations where a design will be used.
3. Go to those locations and observe how people interact. the artifacts in their environment.
4. Develop the prototypes and props that you need to explore an idea. Identify the people, personas and scenarios that may help you with insight into the design directions.,
5. Bodystorm the scenarios.
6. Record the scenarios with video and analyze them for insights.

REFERENCES

Understanding contexts by being there: case studies in bodystorming. Personal and Ubiquitous Computing, Vol. 7, No. 2. (July 2003), pp. 125-134, doi:10.1007/s00779-003-0238-7 by Antti Oulasvirta, Esko Kurvinen, Tomi Kankainen

boundary shifting

WHAT IS IT?

Boundary shifting involves identifying features or ideas outside the boundary of the system related to the defined problem and applying to them to the problem being addressed.

WHY USE THIS METHOD?

1. It is fast and inexpensive.

RESOURCES

1. Pen
2. Paper
3. White board
4. Dry-erase markers

WHEN TO USE THIS METHOD

1. Know Context
2. Know User
3. Frame insights

HOW TO USE THIS METHOD

1. Define the problem.
2. Research outside systems that may have related ideas or problems to the defined problem.
3. Identify ideas or solutions outside the problem system.
4. Apply the outside idea or solution to the problem being addressed.

REFERENCES

1. Walker, D. J., Dagger, B. K. J. and Roy, R. Creative Techniques in Product and Engineering Design. Woodhead Publishing Ltd 1991. ISBN 1 85573 025 1

camera journal

WHAT IS IT?

The research subjects record their activities with a camera and notes. The researcher reviews the images and discusses them with the participants.

WHO INVENTED IT?
WHY USE THIS METHOD?

1. Helps develop empathy for the participants.
2. Participants are involved in the research process.
3. Helps establish rapport with participants.
4. May reveal aspects of life that are seldom seen by outsiders.

CHALLENGES

1. Should obtain informed consent.
2. May not be ideal for research among particularly vulnerable people.
3. May be a relatively expensive research method.
4. May be time consuming.
5. Best used with other methods.
6. Technology may be unreliable.
7. Method may be unpredictable'.
8. Has to be carefully analyzed

WHEN TO USE THIS METHOD

1. Know Context
2. Know User
3. Frame insights

HOW TO USE THIS METHOD

1. Define subject of study
2. Define participants
3. Gather data images and insight statements.
4. Analyze data.
5. Identify insights
6. Rank insights
7. Produce criteria for concept generation from insights.
8. Generate concepts to meet needs of users.

RESOURCES

1. Cameras
2. Voice recorder
3. Video camera
4. Note pad
5. Pens

REFERENCES

1. Latham, A. (2003). Researching and Writing Everyday Accounts ofthe City: An Introduction to the Diary-Photo Diary-interview Method in Knowles, C and Sweetmen, P (eds) Picturing the Social Landscape: Visual Methods and the Sociological Imagination. London, Routledge.
2. Latham,A.R.(2003)'Research, performance, and doing human geography: some reflections on the diary-photo diary-interview method', Environment and Planning A,35(11),1993-2017

closed card sorting

WHAT IS IT?

This is a method for understanding the relationships of a number of pieces of data. Participants asked to arrange individual, unsorted items into groups. A closed sort involves the cards being sorted into groups where the group headings may be defined by the researcher. There are a number of tools available to perform card sorting activities with survey participants via the internet.

Card sorting is applied when:
1. When there is a large number pieces of data.
2. The individual pieces of data are similar.
3. Participants have different perceptions of the data.

WHO INVENTED IT?

Jastrow 1886
Nielsen & Sano 1995

WHY USE THIS METHOD?

1. It is a simple method using index cards,
2. Used to provide insights for interface design.

CHALLENGES

1. Ask participants to fill out a second card if they feel it belongs in two groups.

REFERENCES

1. Jakob Nielsen (May 1995). "Card Sorting to Discover the Users' Model of the Information Space".
2. Jakob Nielsen (July 19, 2004). "Card Sorting: How Many Users to Test".

WHEN TO USE THIS METHOD

1. Know Context
2. Know User
3. Frame insights
4. Explore Concepts

HOW TO USE THIS METHOD

1. Recruit 15 to 20 participants representative of your user group.
2. Provide a deck of cards using words and or images relevant to your concept.
3. Provide clear instructions. Ask your participants to arrange the cards in ways that make sense to them. 100 cards takes about 1 hour to sort.
4. The user sorts labelled cards into groups by under header cards defined by the researcher.
5. The user can generate more card labels.
6. If users do not understand a card ask them to exclude it. Ask participants for their rationale for any dual placements of cards.
7. Discuss why the cards are placed in a particular pile yields insight into user perceptions.
8. Analyze the data. Create a hierarchy for the information
9. Use post cards or post-it notes.

RESOURCES

1. Post cards
2. Pens
3. Post-it-notes
4. Laptop computer
5. A table

case studies: clinical

WHAT IS IT?

A clinical case study is type of case study focuses on an individual person in depth. It often involves detailed interviews and observation.

WHO INVENTED IT?

Frederic Le Play is credited with creating the first case study in 1829

WHY USE THIS METHOD?

1. It is possible to uncover in-depth information.
2. It is flexible.
3. It can be undertaken in many different contexts.
4. It may be inexpensive.

CHALLENGES

1. You cannot generalize on the basis of an individual case
2. It is difficult to develop general theories on the basis of specific cases.
3. The case study has a bias toward confirming the researcher's preconceived notions.
4. Subjectivity
5. Time consuming

REFERENCES

1. Robert E. Stake, The Art of Case Study Research (Thousand Oaks: Sage, 1995). ISBN 0-8039-5767-X

WHEN TO USE THIS METHOD

1. Know Context
2. Know User
3. Frame insights

HOW TO USE THIS METHOD

1. Select the best type of case study for your audience.
2. Review similar case studies
3. Select your participants.
4. Determine whether you will study an individual or a group.
5. Draft a list of questions.
6. Arrange interviews
7. Obtain consent
8. Conduct interviews
9. Analyze the data
10. Create insights
11. Create recommendations.

RESOURCES

1. Note pad
2. Pens
3. Camera
4. Video camera
5. Digital audio recorder
6. Post-it notes

case studies: historical

WHAT IS IT?
Historical case studies follow the development of an individual, an institution, a system, a community, an organization, an event, or a culture over time.

WHO INVENTED IT?
Frederic Le Play is credited with creating the first case study in 1829

WHY USE THIS METHOD?
1. It is possible to uncover in-depth information.
2. It is flexible.
3. It can be undertaken in many different contexts.
4. It may be inexpensive.

CHALLENGES
1. You cannot generalize on the basis of an individual case
2. It is difficult to develop general theories on the basis of specific cases.
3. The case study has a bias toward confirming the researcher's preconceived notions.
4. Subjectivity
5. Time consuming

REFERENCES
1. Robert E. Stake, The Art of Case Study Research (Thousand Oaks: Sage, 1995). ISBN 0-8039-5767-X

WHEN TO USE THIS METHOD
1. Know Context
2. Know User
3. Frame insights

HOW TO USE THIS METHOD
1. Select the best type of case study for your audience.
2. Review similar case studies
3. Select your participants.
4. Determine whether you will study an individual or a group.
5. Draft a list of questions.
6. Arrange interviews
7. Obtain consent
8. Conduct interviews
9. Analyze the data
10. Create insights
11. Create recommendations.

RESOURCES
1. Note pad
2. Pens
3. Camera
4. Video camera
5. Digital audio recorder
6. Post-it notes

case studies: multi case

WHAT IS IT?
A multi-case study is a collection of case studies of an individual, an institution, a system, a community, an organization, an event, or a culture.

WHO INVENTED IT?
Frederic Le Play is credited with creating the first case study in 1829

WHY USE THIS METHOD?
1. It is possible to uncover in-depth information.
2. It is flexible.
3. It can be undertaken in many different contexts.
4. It may be inexpensive.

CHALLENGES
1. You cannot generalize on the basis of an individual case
2. It is difficult to develop general theories on the basis of specific cases.
3. The case study has a bias toward confirming the researcher's preconceived notions.
4. Subjectivity
5. Time consuming

Image Copyright Igor Dutina, 2013
Used under license from Shutterstock.com

WHEN TO USE THIS METHOD
1. Know Context
2. Know User
3. Frame insights

HOW TO USE THIS METHOD
1. Select the best type of case study for your audience.
2. Review similar case studies
3. Select your participants.
4. Determine whether you will study an individual or a group.
5. Draft a list of questions.
6. Arrange interviews
7. Obtain consent
8. Conduct interviews
9. Analyze the data
10. Create insights
11. Create recommendations.

RESOURCES
1. Note pad
2. Pens
3. Camera
4. Video camera
5. Digital audio recorder
6. Post-it notes

REFERENCES
1. Robert E. Stake, The Art of Case Study Research (Thousand Oaks: Sage, 1995). ISBN 0-8039-5767-X
2. "Case Study," in Norman K. Denzin and Yvonna S. Lincoln, eds., The Sage Handbook of Qualitative Research, 4th Edition (Thousand Oaks, CA: Sage),

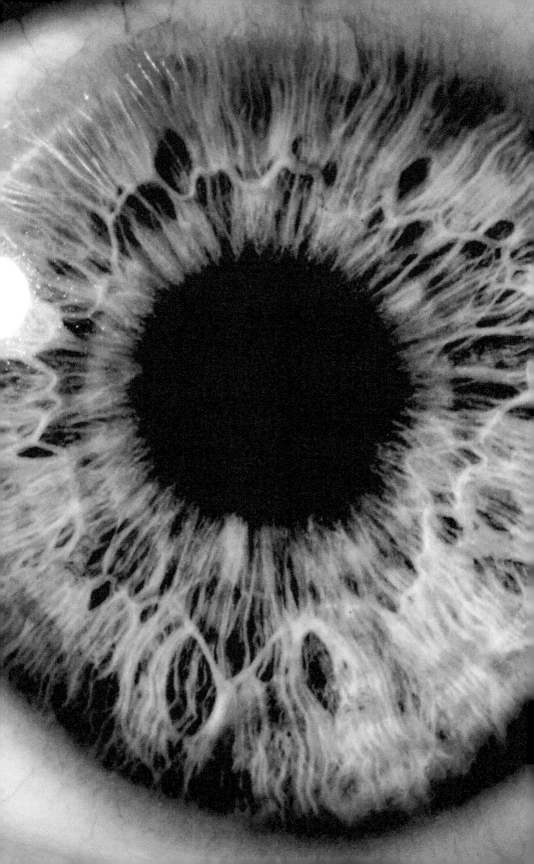

case studies: observational

WHAT IS IT?
Observational case studies focus on observing an individual, an institution, a system, a community,an organization, an event, or a culture.

WHO INVENTED IT?
Frederic Le Play is credited with creating the first case study in 1829

WHY USE THIS METHOD?
1. It is possible to uncover in-depth information.
2. It is flexible.
3. It can be undertaken in many different contexts.
4. It may be inexpensive.

CHALLENGES
1. You cannot generalize on the basis of an individual case
2. It is difficult to develop general theories on the basis of specific cases.
3. The case study has a bias toward confirming the researcher's preconceived notions.
4. Subjectivity
5. Time consuming

WHEN TO USE THIS METHOD
1. Know Context
2. Know User
3. Frame insights

HOW TO USE THIS METHOD
1. Select the best type of case study for your audience.
2. Review similar case studies
3. Select your participants.
4. Determine whether you will study an individual or a group.
5. Obtain consent
6. Conduct observations
7. Analyze the data
8. Create insights
9. Create recommendations.

RESOURCES
1. Note pad
2. Pens
3. Camera
4. Video camera
5. Digital audio recorder
6. Post-it notes

REFERENCES
1. Robert E. Stake, The Art of Case Study Research (Thousand Oaks: Sage, 1995). ISBN 0-8039-5767-X
2. "Case Study," in Norman K. Denzin and Yvonna S. Lincoln, eds., The Sage Handbook of Qualitative Research, 4th Edition (Thousand Oaks, CA: Sage),

case studies: oral history

WHAT IS IT?

Oral case studies are case studies narrated by one person speaking for and about themselves. This allows communication of their point of view. The narrator may or may not be aware of the full context of their experiences.

WHO INVENTED IT?

Frederic Le Play is credited with creating the first case study in 1829

WHY USE THIS METHOD?

1. It is possible to uncover in-depth information.
2. It is flexible.
3. It can be undertaken in many different contexts.
4. It may be inexpensive.

CHALLENGES

1. You cannot generalize on the basis of an individual case
2. It is difficult to develop general theories on the basis of specific cases.
3. The case study has a bias toward confirming the researcher's preconceived notions.
4. Subjectivity
5. Time consuming

Image Copyright dundanim, 2013
Used under license from Shutterstock.com

WHEN TO USE THIS METHOD

1. Know Context
2. Know User
3. Frame insights

HOW TO USE THIS METHOD

1. Select the best type of case study for your audience.
2. Review similar case studies
3. Select your participants.
4. Determine whether you will study an individual or a group.
5. Draft a list of questions.
6. Arrange interviews
7. Conduct interviews
8. Analyze the data
9. Create insights
10. Create recommendations.

RESOURCES

1. Note pad
2. Pens
3. Camera
4. Video camera
5. Digital audio recorder
6. Post-it notes

REFERENCES

1. Robert E. Stake, The Art of Case Study Research (Thousand Oaks: Sage, 1995). ISBN 0-8039-5767-X
2. "Case Study," in Norman K. Denzin and Yvonna S. Lincoln, eds., The Sage Handbook of Qualitative Research, 4th Edition (Thousand Oaks, CA: Sage),

case studies: situational

WHAT IS IT?

This form studies particular events. The view of all participants in the event are sought

WHO INVENTED IT?

Frederic Le Play is credited with creating the first case study in 1829

WHY USE THIS METHOD?

1. It is possible to uncover in-depth information.
2. It is flexible.
3. It can be undertaken in many different contexts.
4. It may be inexpensive.

CHALLENGES

1. You cannot generalize on the basis of an individual case
2. It is difficult to develop general theories on the basis of specific cases.
3. The case study has a bias toward confirming the researcher's preconceived notions.
4. Subjectivity
5. Time consuming

REFERENCES

1. Robert E. Stake, The Art of Case Study Research (Thousand Oaks: Sage, 1995). ISBN 0-8039-5767-X
2. "Case Study," in Norman K. Denzin and Yvonna S. Lincoln, eds., The Sage Handbook of Qualitative Research, 4th Edition (Thousand Oaks, CA: Sage),

WHEN TO USE THIS METHOD

1. Know Context
2. Know User
3. Frame insights

HOW TO USE THIS METHOD

1. Select the best type of case study for your audience.
2. Review similar case studies
3. Select your participants.
4. Determine whether you will study an individual or a group.
5. Draft a list of questions.
6. Arrange interviews
7. Obtain consent
8. Conduct interviews
9. Analyze the data
10. Create insights
11. Create recommendations.

RESOURCES

1. Note pad
2. Pens
3. Camera
4. Video camera
5. Digital audio recorder
6. Post-it notes

close ended questions

WHAT IS IT?
Close ended questions are questions that can be answered with simple yes or no responses or a specific answer that doesn't need to be interpreted. Also called dichotomous or saturated questions.

Some examples are:
1. Shall we continue?
2. Is this correct?
3. What is this color?

WHY USE THIS METHOD?
1. Fast
2. Easy to analyze answers

CHALLENGES
1. Should be used in an interview to clarify responses.
2. Should be combined with open ended questions.
3. Can be leading.
4. Open-ended questions develop trust
5. Perceived as more threatening than open ended questions.
6. A closed question may be impossible to answer such as "Have you stopped taking cocaine?"

WHEN TO USE THIS METHOD
1. Know Context
2. Know User

HOW TO USE THIS METHOD
1. If people stop responding to open questions ask close ended questions to restart conversation.
2. Multiple choice questions are a form of closed question.

RESOURCES
1. Pen
2. Paper
3. Video camera
4. Question guide
5. Digital voice recorder
6. Questionnaires
7. Surveys

REFERENCES
1. Dillman D., Smyth J., & Christioan LM. (2009) Internet and Mixed-Mode Surveys. The Tailored Design Method. John Wiley & Sons. New Jersey.
2. Howard Schuman and Stanley Presser (October 1979). "The Open and Closed Question". American Sociological Review 44 (5): 692–712.

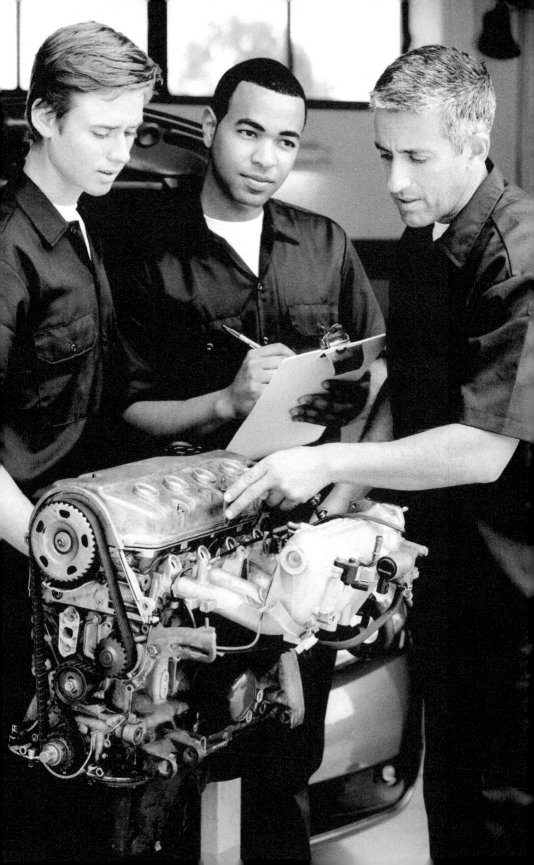

coaching method

WHAT IS IT?

An expert coaches the participant. The expert answers the participant's questions while a researcher observes the participant's interaction with the product or service.

WHY USE THIS METHOD?

1. The method prototypes the user interaction with the system.
2. Information obtained can be used to refine the design or documentation.

WHEN TO USE THIS METHOD

1. Know Context
2. Know User
3. Frame insights
4. Explore Concepts

HOW TO USE THIS METHOD

1. Select the participants
2. Select the tasks and design scenarios.
3. Ask the participant to perform the interaction with the expert coach.
4. During the interaction the participant will ask the expert questions about the interaction.
5. Video and record the questions and interactions.
6. Refine the design based on the questions and interactions.

RESOURCES

1. Video camera
2. Computers

REFERENCES

1. J. Nielsen "Usability Engineering", pp.199-200, Academic Press, 1993

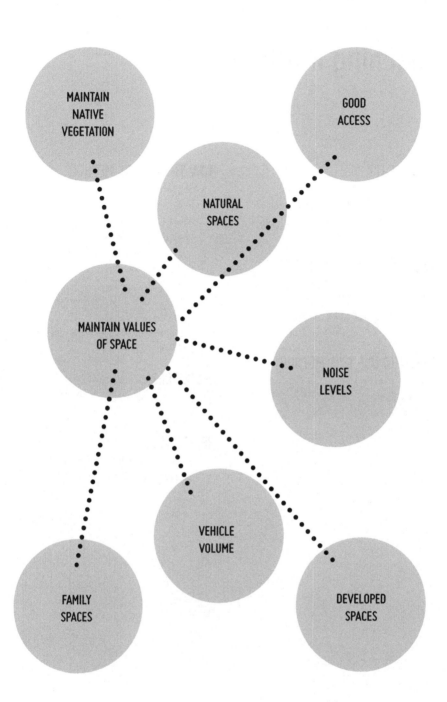

MAINTAIN
NATIVE
VEGETATION

GOOD
ACCESS

NATURAL
SPACES

MAINTAIN VALUES
OF SPACE

NOISE
LEVELS

FAMILY
SPACES

VEHICLE
VOLUME

DEVELOPED
SPACES

cognitive map

WHAT IS IT?
A cognitive map is a mental map of an environment. Cognitive maps are a method by which people remember and recall a physical or virtual environment and spatial knowledge.

WHO INVENTED IT?
Edward Tolman 1948.
Trowbridge 1913

WHY USE THIS METHOD?
1. Useful to discover how people navigate in a real or virtual space.
2. Used to understand a problem space.
3. Cognitive maps uncover how people make decisions.
4. Cognitive maps uncover how people perceive spaces

WHEN TO USE THIS METHOD
1. Know Context
2. Know User
3. Frame insights
4. Explore Concepts

SEE ALSO
1. Mind maps

HOW TO USE THIS METHOD
1. Ask a subject to create a map showing how they navigate in a real or a virtual space.
2. Select participants
3. Ask the participant to describe how they get to a location and how they return referencing the obstacles.
4. Maps can be created by a group of people to incorporate different viewpoints.

RESOURCES
1. Note pad
2. Paper
3. Pens
4. Video camera

REFERENCES
5. Eden, C. (1992). On the nature of cognitive maps. Journal of Management Studies, 29, 261-265.
6. Kitchin RM (1994). "Cognitive Maps: What Are They and Why Study Them?". Journal of Environmental Psychology 14 (1): 1—19. DOI:10.1016/S0272-4944(05)80194-X.
1. Tolman E.C. (July 1948). "Cognitive maps in rats and men". Psychological Review 55 (4): 189—208. DOI:10.1037/h0061626. PMID 18870876.

cognitive task analysis

WHAT IS IT?
The purpose of a cognitive task analysis is to define the decision requirements and psychological processes used by expert individuals. Task analysis makes it possible to design and develop strategy for tasks related to a system or service being designed.

Factors analyzed could include:
1. Task duration and variability
2. Task frequency
3. Task sequence
4. Task allocation
5. Task complexity
6. Environmental conditions
7. Data and information dependencies
8. Tools needed for the activity
9. User knowledge and skills.

WHO INVENTED IT?
IBM circa 1985

WHY USE THIS METHOD?
1. Generates detailed data
2. Analyze the participant's perceptions and motivations related to tasks.

CHALLENGES
1. Can be time intensive and costly.

Photo: photocase.com – daumenkino

WHEN TO USE THIS METHOD
1. Define intent
2. Know Context
3. Know User
4. Frame insights
5. Explore Concepts

HOW TO USE THIS METHOD
1. Develop some general understanding of the domain area in which the cognitive task analysis will be conducted.
2. Identify experts
3. Identify the activity's knowledge structures with observations and interviews
4. Develop a strategy for each of the tasks.
5. Analyze and verify data

RESOURCES
1. Computers
2. Workstations
3. Video Cameras
4. White board
5. Notebook
6. Pens

REFERENCES
1. Crandall, B., Klein, G., and Hoffman, R. (2006). Working minds: A practitioner's guide to cognitive task analysis. MIT Press.
2. Kirwan, B. and Ainsworth, L. (Eds.) (1992). A guide to task analysis. Taylor and Francis.

collage

WHAT IS IT?

A collage involves gluing images or words onto paper. Research participants are given a large and diverse supply of images and words. The images and words chosen should be abstract so as not to influence the participants too much but may include images of objects and people and interactions. The moderator provides the participants with guidelines for the activity. They are a useful medium for communicating emotions and ideas and starting a conversation.

WHO INVENTED IT?

Invented in China, around 200 BC
Pablo Picasso and Georges Braque 1912
The word cllages comes from the French word "coller" which means to glue.

WHY USE THIS METHOD?

1. Collages can enhance discourse, illustrate theses, and to anchor scientific observations in human experience.
2. The creation of a collage is a process that is both creative and analytical.
3. Collages can provide clues to the researcher about the participants lifestyle, aesthetic likes and dislikes.
4. A collage can give direction in selecting colors for a manufactured product
5. Collages are very suitable to present a particular atmosphere or context that you want to capture in the form of the new product ideas and concepts.

Image Copyright Leigh Prather, 2013 Used under license from Shutterstock.com

WHEN TO USE THIS METHOD

1. Know Context
2. Know User
3. Frame insights
4. Explore Concepts

HOW TO USE THIS METHOD

1. Define the theme.
2. Define the scope of the study such as number of words or images.
3. Print words and images onto sticker sheets.
4. Distribute scissors.
5. Group creates collages.
6. Subjects tell own stories through the collages.
7. Collect the stories.
8. Analyze the stories.

RESOURCES

1. Scissors
2. Magazines or preprinted stickers
3. Paper
4. Glue

REFERENCES

1. Brandon Taylor. Urban walls : a generation of collage in Europe & America : Burhan Dogançay with François Dufrêne, Raymond Hains, Robert Rauschenberg, Mimmo Rotella, Jacques Villeglé, Wolf Vostell ISBN 978-1-55595-288-4; ISBN 1-55595-288-7New York : Hudson Hills Press ; [Lanham, MD] : Distributed in the United States by National Book Network, 2008

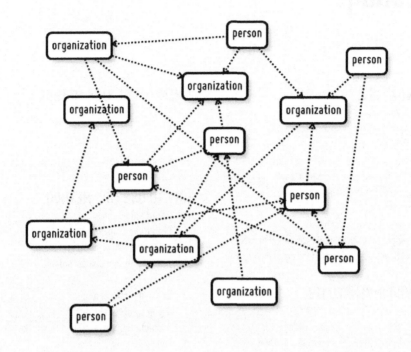

It is possible to show existing and planned relationships on your communications map

communications map

WHAT IS IT?

A communications map is a tool to study and create strategy for communications. It may be used in a project to understand where there are gaps which could affect the project outcomes. The project communication map processes documents the critical links among people and information that are necessary for successful project outcomes.

WHY USE THIS METHOD?

1. It may show where there are gaps in communications which need to be addressed.
2. Assists the project team to provide timely and accurate information to all stakeholders.

WHEN TO USE THIS METHOD

1. Know Context
2. Know User
3. Frame insights

RESOURCES

1. Pens
2. Paper
3. White board
4. Dry-erase markers

HOW TO USE THIS METHOD

1. Identify stakeholders.
2. Identify those with whom
3. Your organization needs the strongest communications linkages.
4. Identify Internal audiences.
5. Identify Peer groups or sub groups.
6. Identify Strong and frequent communications
7. Connectivity needed to a primary audience.
8. Identify less frequent communications connectivity needed to a secondary audience.
9. Determine stakeholder needs.
10. Identify communication methods and resources.
11. Prepare communication map showing existing and desired communications.
12. Distribute to stakeholders for feedback.
13. Incorporate Changes
14. Implement.

CONJOINT ANALYSIS

Please rate how you like these types of cheese

	I really dislike it	I do not like it	Neutral	I like it	I like it a lot
Cheddar	☐	☐	☐	☐	☐
Stilton	☐	☐	☐	☐	☐
Danish Blue	☐	☐	☐	☐	☐
Gorgonzola	☐	☐	☐	☐	☐

conjoint analysis

WHAT IS IT?
Conjoint analysis is a method to gain insight into how people value features or components of a product , service or experience. It can be used to decide features a new product should have and how a new product should be priced.

WHO INVENTED IT?
Paul Green University of Pennsylvania.
V. "Seenu" Srinivasan Stanford University

WHY USE THIS METHOD?
1. Uncovers perceptions that the respondent may not be consciously aware of.
2. Can use physical objects.
3. Attempts to measure psychological trade-offs when evaluating several attributes together
4. Can be carried out telephone or face-to-face.

CHALLENGES
1. Studies can be complex

RESOURCES
1. Paper
2. Pens
3. Phone
4. Questionnaires
5. Software

WHEN TO USE THIS METHOD
1. Define intent
2. Know Context
3. Know User
4. Frame insights

HOW TO USE THIS METHOD
1. The respondent is shown a number of features sometimes in pairs
2. The respondent rates or chooses combinations of features.
3. The data is analyzed and the features ranked.
4. Mathematical models are used to determine the respondent's product or service of choice.

REFERENCES
1. Green, P. and Srinivasan, V. (1978) Conjoint analysis in consumer research: Issues and outlook, Journal of Consumer Research, vol 5, September 1978, pp 103-123.
2. Orme, B. (2005) Getting Started with Conjoint Analysis Madison, WI: Research Publishers LLC. ISBN 0-9727297-4-7
3. Louviere, Jordan J. "Conjoint Analysis Modelling of Stated Preferences: A Review of Theory, Methods, Recent Developments and External Validity." Journal of Transport Economics and Policy, Vol. 22, No. 1, Stated Preference Methods in Transport Research (Jan., 1988), pp. 93-119.

cradle to cradle

WHAT IS IT?

Cradle-to-Cradle is is a biometic approach to the design of products and systems proposed by the authors William McDonough and Michael Braungart based on the intelligence of natural systems. it is an industrial and social framework that proposes systems that are efficient and waste free.

The basis for the Cradle-to-Cradle approach involves three guiding principles:

1 Use current solar income.
2 Waste equals Food.
3 Celebrate diversity.

WHO INVENTED IT?

William McDonough and Michael Braungart 2002

WHY USE THIS METHOD?

1. The Cradle-to-Cradle approach is a framework for global economic and natural stainability

CHALLENGES

1. Cradle to Cradle is often criticized for its lack of attention to energy.
2. Some critics see the approach as utopian.
3. Even the highest Cradle to cradle certification requires only 50 % of energy for production to come from solar sources.

WHEN TO USE THIS METHOD

1. Define intent
2. Know Context
3. Know User
4. Frame insights
5. Explore Concepts
6. Make Plans
7. Deliver Offering

HOW TO USE THIS METHOD

1. Do not specify environmentally damaging materials processes and systems.
2. Follow informed personal preferences.
3. Create a 'passive positive' list of substances known to be healthy and safe for use.
4. Eliminate waste
5. Use solar energy.
6. Respect human and natural systems.
7. Design the product from beginning to end to become food for either biological or technical metabolisms.
8. Reinvent. Recast the design assignment. Towards environmentally sustainable ends.

REFERENCES

Braungart, Michael; & McDonough, William (2002). Cradle to Cradle: Remaking the Way We Make Things. North Point Press. ISBN 0-86547-587-3.

Photo: photocase.com – alwayshappy

cultural immersion

WHAT IS IT?

The design team spends a period of time exploring a location or environment to gain a deeper understanding of the design context.

WHY USE THIS METHOD?

1. To gain a deeper understanding of the design context
2. To gain empathy

RESOURCES

1. Note book
2. Digital camera
3. Video Camera
4. Digital Voice recorder

WHEN TO USE THIS METHOD

Most often used in the early stages of a design process

HOW TO USE THIS METHOD

Activities may involve

1. Interviews
2. Photography
3. Observations
4. Video
5. Note taking
6. Sketching
7. Recordings
8. Collecting objects.

cultural inventory

WHAT IS IT?
It is a survey focused on the cultural assets of a location or organization.

WHO INVENTED IT?
Julian Haynes Steward may have been the first to use the term in 1947.

WHY USE THIS METHOD?
1. Can be used in strategic planning
2. Can be used to solve problems.

CHALLENGES
1. Requires time and resources

WHEN TO USE THIS METHOD
1. Know Context
2. Know User
3. Frame insights
4. Explore Concepts

HOW TO USE THIS METHOD
1. Create your team
2. Collect existing research
3. Review existing research and identify gaps
4. Host a meeting of stakeholders
5. Promote the meeting
6. Ask open-ended questions about the culture and heritage
7. Set a time limit of 2 hours for the meeting.
8. Plan the collection phase
9. Compile inventory. This can be in the form of a web site
10. Distribute the inventory and obtain feedback.

RESOURCES
1. Diary
2. Notebooks
3. Pens
4. Post-it notes
5. Voice recorder
6. Post cards
7. Digital Camera

REFERENCES
1. Spradley, James P. Participant Observation. Holt, Rinehart and Winston, 1980.

cultural probes

WHAT IS IT?

A cultural probe is a method of collecting information about people, their context and their culture. The aim of this method is to record events, behaviors and interactions in their context. This method involves the participants to record and collect the data themselves.

WHO INVENTED IT?

Bill Gaver Royal College of Art London 1969

WHY USE THIS METHOD?

1. This is a useful method when the participants that are being studied are hard to reach for example if they are travelling.
2. It is a useful technique if the activities being studied take place over an extended period or at irregular intervals.
3. The information collected can be used to build personas.

CHALLENGES

4. It is important with this method to select the participants carefully and give them support during the study.

SEE ALSO

1. Diary study

WHEN TO USE THIS METHOD

1. Define intent
2. Know Context
3. Know User
4. Frame insights

HOW TO USE THIS METHOD

1. Define the objective of your study.
2. Recruit your participants.
3. Brief the participants
4. Supply participants with kit. The items in the kit are selected to collect the type of information you want to gather and can include items such as notebooks, diary, camera, voice recorder or post cards.
5. You can use an affinity diagram to analyze the data collected

RESOURCES

1. Diary
2. Notebooks
3. Pens
4. Post-it notes
5. Voice recorder
6. Post cards
7. Digital Camera

REFERENCES

1. Bailey, Kathleen M. (1990) The use of diary studies in teacher education programs In Richards, J. C. & Nunan, D. (org.). Second Language Teacher Education (pp. 215-226). Cambridge: Cambridge University Press.

customer experience audit

WHAT IS IT?

A customer experience audit is a method of systematically analyzing an organization's with their customers. It is a systematic way of understanding how your customers see your organization.

WHY USE THIS METHOD?

1. Increase employee engagement
2. Establish a baseline of Customer Experience
3. Provide insights into opportunities
4. Prepare a team for Customer Journey Mapping
5. Reveal customer perspective to employees
6. A customer perspective allows your organization to shift its culture from opinion to
7. Fact based thinking.
8. Audit findings get people on the same page.

CHALLENGES

1. When your customer experience has evolved over time, rather than being intentionally designed, product and company performance suffer.
2. Which customers are your most valuable
3. Which interactions these key customers most value

Image Copyright LuckyPhoto, 2013 Used under license from Shutterstock.com

WHEN TO USE THIS METHOD

1. Know Context
2. Know User
3. Frame insights

HOW TO USE THIS METHOD

Will depend on your organization anf customer base, but could typically include;

1. Customer surveys and interviews with; existing and past customers as well as potential customers
2. Mystery shopping
3. Focus groups
4. Interviews with staff who interact with your customers.
5. Review of customer interactions and literature including face-to-face interviews, telephone and online surveys
6. Prospective, current, and lost customers.
7. Signs
8. Advertisements
9. Website
10. E-mail or Newsletters
11. Facebook or other social pages
12. Retail Space
13. Marketing Materials
14. Information Forms

REFERENCES

1. Rubin, Herbert and Irene Rubin. Qualitative Interviewing: The Art of Hearing Data. 2nd edition. Thousand Oaks, CA: Sage Publications, 2004. Print.
2. Kvale, Steinar. Interviews: An Introduction to Qualitative Research Interviewing, Sage Publications, 1996

	ANTICIPATE	ENTER	ENGAGE	EXIT	REVIEW
CUSTOMER MORE POSITIVE EXPERIENCES					
CUSTOMER POSITIVE EXPERIENCES					
BASELINE					
CUSTOMER NEGATIVE EXPERIENCES					
CUSTOMER MORE NEGATIVE EXPERIENCES					
EMOTIONAL EXPERIENCE					

customer experience map

WHAT IS IT?

Customer experience also called customer journey mapping is a method of documenting and visualizing the experiences that customers have as they use a product or service and their responses to their experiences.

It allows your team to access and analyze the interacting factors that form a customer experience.

WHY USE THIS METHOD?

1. Helps develop a consistent, predictable customer experience,
2. Presents an overview of your customer's experience from their point of view.
3. Helps reduce the number of dissatisfied customers
4. Can be used with different personas.

WHEN TO USE THIS METHOD

1. Know Context
2. Know User
3. Frame insights

HOW TO USE THIS METHOD

1. Identify your team.
2. Identify the customer experience to be analyzed. Identify the context. Identify personas.
3. Define the experience as a time line with stages such as anticipation, entry, engagement, exit, and reflection.
4. Use post-it notes to add positive and negative experiences to the relevant parts of the time line.
5. Order the experiences around a baseline by how positive or negative the experience were.
6. Analyze the parts of the time line and activities that have the most negative experiences. These are opportunities for design.

RESOURCES

1. Post-it-notes
2. Printed or projected template
3. White board
4. Markers

REFERENCES

1. Joshi, Hetal. "Customer Journey Mapping: The Road to Success." Cognizant. (2009) Web. 26 Jul. 2013.
2. World Class Skills Programme. "Customer Journey Mapping." Developing Responsive Provision. (2006): n. page. Web. 27 Jul. 2013.

customer first questions

WHAT IS IT?
Customer first questions predict the reaction of customers to a new product or service.

WHO INVENTED IT?
Edith Wilson, Hewlett-Packard,

WHY USE THIS METHOD?
1. To identify customer needs and desires.
2. To reduce the risk of product development
3. To reduce the number of product design changes during the development process.
4. The Customer first questions method has been used by many large organizations

WHEN TO USE THIS METHOD
1. Define intent
2. Know Context
3. Know User
4. Frame insights

HOW TO USE THIS METHOD
1. Brainstorm the most appropriate research methods.
   ◦ What customer problems does our product/service solve that our competitors do not?
   ◦ What benefits does our product/service offer that our competitors do not?
   ◦ What motivates the customer to purchase our product/service over that of our competitors?
2. Identify using research the needs and desires of customers.
3. Analyze how the product satisfies these needs and desired and how this compares to competitor's products.
4. Analyze whether customers will prefer the product to competitor's products.

RESOURCES
1. Paper
2. Pens
3. White board
4. Dry erase markers

CUSTOMER NEEDS MATRIX

	CUSTOMER DEMOGRAPHICS	CUSTOMER NEEDS	USAGE				
			WHO	WHAT	WHEN	WHERE	HOW
1							
2							
3							
4							
5							
6							
7							
8							
9							
10							
11							
12							

customer needs matrix

WHAT IS IT?

The customer needs table helps integrated product development teams (IPDT) translate customer needs and wants into required designs that may meet customer expectations prior to the potential development of new products or service development.

WHY USE THIS METHOD?

1. To uncover customer needs and desires
2. To translate customer needs and desires into product features.
3. To reduce changes necessary during product development.

RESOURCES

1. Paper
2. Pens
3. White board
4. Dry erase markers

WHEN TO USE THIS METHOD

1. Define intent
2. Know Context
3. Know User
4. Frame insights

HOW TO USE THIS METHOD

1. The design team selects methods for collecting data.
2. Data collection methods : Customer surveys, interviews, focus groups, benchmarks, similar product data, summarized studies, product demos, and others.
3. A sample of customers is selected and interviewed in relation to the factors listed on the customer needs matrix.
4. The responses are entered into the table.
5. The table is reviewed by the team.
6. The team creates a list of insights.

day in the life

WHAT IS IT?
A study in which the designer observes the participant in the location and context of their usual activities, observing and recording events to understand the activities from the participant's point of view. This is sometimes repeated. Mapping a 'Day in the Life' as a storyboard can provide a focus for discussion.

WHO INVENTED IT?
ALex Bavelas 1944

WHY USE THIS METHOD?
1. This method informs the design process by observation of real activities and behaviors.
2. This method provides insights with relatively little cost and time.

CHALLENGES
1. Choose the participants carefully
2. Document everything. Something that seems insignificant may become significant later.

WHEN TO USE THIS METHOD
1. Know Context
2. Know User
3. Frame insights

HOW TO USE THIS METHOD
1. Define activities to study
2. Recruit participants
3. Prepare
4. Observe subjects in context.
5. Capture data,
6. Create storyboard with text and timeline.
7. Analyze data
8. Create insights.
9. Identify issues
10. Identify needs
11. Add new/more requirements to concept development

RESOURCES
1. Camera
2. Notebook
3. Video camera
4. Voice recorder
5. Pens

REFERENCES
1. Shadowing: And Other Techniques for Doing Fieldwork in Modern Societies [Paperback] Barbara Czarniawska. Publisher: Copenhagen Business School Pr (December 2007) ISBN-10: 8763002159 ISBN-13: 978-8763002158

Photo: photocase.com – froodmat

diary study

WHAT IS IT?
This method involves participants recording specific events, feelings or interactions, in a diary supplied by the researcher. User Diaries help provide insight into behavior. Participants record their behavior and thoughts. Diaries can uncover behavior that may not be articulated in an interview or easily visible to outsiders.

WHO INVENTED IT?
Gordon Allport, may have been the first to describe diary studies in 1942.

WHY USE THIS METHOD?
1. Can capture data that is difficult to capture using other methods.
2. Useful when you wish to gather information and minimize your influence on research subjects.
3. When the process or event you're exploring takes place intermittently or
4. When the process or event you're exploring takes place over a long period.

CHALLENGES
1. Process can be expensive and time consuming.
2. Needs participant monitoring.
3. Diary can fit into users' pocket.
4. It is difficult to get materials back.

WHEN TO USE THIS METHOD
1. Know Context
2. Know User
3. Frame insights

HOW TO USE THIS METHOD
1. A diary can be kept over a period of one week or longer.
2. Define focus for the study.
3. Recruit participants carefully.
4. Decide method: preprinted, diary notebook or online.
5. Prepare diary packs. Can be preprinted sheets or blank 20 page notebooks with prepared questions or online web based diary.
6. Brief participants.
7. Distribute diaries directly or by mail.
8. Conduct study. Keep in touch with participants.
9. Conduct debrief interview.
10. Look for insights.

RESOURCES
1. Diary
2. Preprinted diary sheets
3. Online diary
4. Pens
5. Disposable cameras
6. Digital camera
7. Self addressed envelopes

REFERENCES
1. Bailey, Kathleen M. (1990) The use of diary studies in teacher education programs In Richards, J. C. & Nunan, D. (org.). Second Language Teacher Education (pp. 215-226). Cambridge: Cambridge University Press.

SEE ALSO
Empathy probe

day experience method

WHAT IS IT?

The method requires participants to record answers to questions at during a day. The person's mobile phone is used to prompt them The participants use a notebook, a camera and a voice recorder to answer your questions. the interviews are followed by a focus group.

WHO INVENTED IT?

Intille 2003

WHY USE THIS METHOD?

1. The participants are co-researchers.
2. Reduces the influence of the researcher on the participant when compared to methods such as interviews or direct observation.

CHALLENGES

1. Cost of devices.
2. This method should be used with other methods.

WHEN TO USE THIS METHOD

1. Know Context
2. Know User
3. Frame insights

HOW TO USE THIS METHOD

1. Conduct a preliminary survey to focus the method on preferred questions.
2. Recruit participants.
3. The experience sampling takes place over one day.
4. The participants are asked to provide answers to questions at irregular intervals when promoted by a SMS message via the participant's mobile phone.
5. The interval can be 60 to 90 minutes.
6. The participant can record the activity with a camera, notebook or voice recorder.
7. Soon after the day organize a focus group with the participants.
8. The participants describe their day using the recorded material.

RESOURCES

1. Mobile phone
2. Automated SMS messaging
3. Notebook
4. Camera
5. Software

REFERENCES

1. Hektner, J.M., Schmidt, J.A. & Csikszentmihalyi, M (2006). Experience Sampling Method: Measuring the Quality of Everyday Life, London: Sage.
2. Kahneman, D., Krueger, A. B., Schkade, D. A., Schwarz, N., & Stone, A. A. (2004). 'A Survey Method for Characterizing Daily Life Experience: The Day Reconstruction Method'. Science, 306(5702), 1776-1780.

DEMING CYCLE

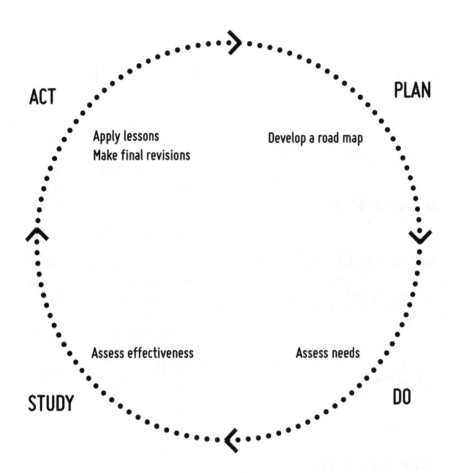

ACT

Apply lessons
Make final revisions

PLAN

Develop a road map

STUDY

Assess effectiveness

DO

Assess needs

deming cycle

WHAT IS IT?

The Deming Cycle is a method to test information before making a decision for the continuous improvement of systems and products. Also known as PDCA and Shewhart cycle. A principal of the method is iteration.

WHO INVENTED IT?

Made popular by Dr. W. Edwards Deming based on the "scientific method"of Francis Bacon *Novum Organum, 1620*

WHY USE THIS METHOD?

1. To assess proposed problem solutions
2. To identify and measure the effects and outcomes of initial, trial efforts.

RESOURCES

1. Paper
2. Pens
3. White board
4. Dry erase markers

WHEN TO USE THIS METHOD

1. Frame insights
2. Explore Concepts

HOW TO USE THIS METHOD

Plan. Establish objectives.
Do. Implement the plan.
Check. Study the results and compare to the expected results.
Act. On differences between planned and actual results.

REFERENCES

1. Rother, Mike (2010). Toyota Kata. Chapter 6: MGraw-Hill. ISBN 978-0-07-163523-3.

design workshops

WHAT IS IT?

A design workshop is a strategic design method that involves bringing the design team together with stakeholders to explore issue related to explore issues related to the people who are being designed for or to create design solutions.

WHY USE THIS METHOD?

1. Fast and inexpensive.
2. Increased probability of implementation.
3. Stakeholders can share information.
4. Promotes trust.

CHALLENGES

1. Managing workflow can be challenging.
2. Stakeholders may have conflicting visions.

WHEN TO USE THIS METHOD

1. Know Context
2. Know User
3. Frame insights
4. Explore Concepts

HOW TO USE THIS METHOD

1. See charettes and creative toolkits.

RESOURCES

1. Paper flip chart
2. White board
3. Colored markers
4. Cards
5. Masking tape
6. Rolls of butcher paper
7. Post-it notes
8. Adhesive dots
9. Glue
10. Pins
11. Pens
12. Scissors
13. Spray adhesive
14. Screen
15. Laptop
16. Projector
17. Extension leads
18. Video Camera
19. Digital Camera
20. Chairs
21. Tables

design charette

WHAT IS IT?

A design charette is a collaborative design workshop usually held over one day or several days. Charettes are a fast way of generating ideas while involving diverse stakeholders in your decision process. Charettes have many different structures and often involve multiple sessions. The group divides into smaller groups. The smaller groups present to the larger group.

WHO INVENTED IT?

The French word, "charrette" spelt with two r's means "cart" This use of the term is said to originate from the École des Beaux Arts in Paris during the 19th century, where a cart, collected final drawings while students finished their work.

WHY USE THIS METHOD?

1. Fast and inexpensive.
2. Increased probability of implementation.
3. Stakeholders can share information.
4. Promotes trust.

CHALLENGES

1. Managing workflow can be challenging.
2. Stakeholders may have conflicting visions.

WHEN TO USE THIS METHOD

1. Define intent
2. Know context and user
3. Frame insights
4. Explore concepts
5. Make Plans

RESOURCES

1. Large space
2. Tables
3. Chairs
4. White boards
5. Dry-erase markers
6. Camera
7. Post-it-notes

REFERENCES

1. Day, C. (2003). Consensus Design: Socially Inclusive Process. Oxford, UK, and Burlington, MA: Elsevier Science, Architectural Press.

workshops: creative toolkits

WHAT IS IT?

Collections of modular objects that can be used for participatory modeling and prototyping to inform and inspire design teams. Often used in creative codesign workshops. It is a generative design method which facilitates creative play. The elements can be reused in a number of research sessions in different geographic locations.

WHO INVENTED IT?

Pioneered by Liz Sanders and Lego Johan Roos and Bart Victor 1990s.

WHY USE THIS METHOD?

Helps develop:
1. Problem solving
2. Change management
3. Strategic thinking
4. Decision making
5. Services, product and experience redesign
6. Can be fun
7. Identify opportunities
8. Re frame challenges
9. Leverages creative thinking of the team

WHEN TO USE THIS METHOD
1. Know Context
2. Know User
3. Frame insights
4. Explore Concepts

image: © Grandeduc | Dreamstime.com

HOW TO USE THIS METHOD
1. Form cross-disciplinary team 5 to 20 members. It's best to have teams of not more than 8
2. Identify design problem. Create agenda.
3. Start with a warming up exercise.
4. Write design problem in visible location such as white board.
5. Workshop participants first build individual prototypes exploring the problem.
6. Divide larger group into smaller work groups of 3 to 5 participants.
7. Ask each participant to develop between 1 and design solutions. Can use post-it notes or cards.
8. Through internal discussion each group should select their preferred group design solution.
9. The group builds a collective model incorporating the individual contributions.
10. Each group build a physical model of preferred solution and presents it to larger group.
11. Larger group selects their preferred design solutions by discussion and voting.
12. Capture process and ideas with video or photographs.
13. Debriefing and harvest of ideas.

REFERENCES

1. Statler, M., Roos, J., and B. Victor, 2009, 'Ain't Misbehavin': Taking Play Seriously in Organizations,' Journal of Change Management, 9(1): 87-107.

0.5 day product design charette

HOW TO USE THIS METHOD

1. Choose a problem to focus on.
2. Select moderator.
3. Select and invite participants.
4. Team size of 4 to 20 participants preferred representing users, managers, design and diverse group of stakeholders.
5. Break down teams over 8 into smaller groups of 4 or 5 participants.
6. Brief participants in advance by e-mail.
7. Allow one hour per problem
8. Use creative space such as a room with a large table and whiteboard.
9. Brief participants allow 15 minutes to one hour for individual concept exploration.
10. Give participants a goal such as 5 concepts.
11. Output can be sketches or simple models using materials such as cardboard or toy construction kits.
12. Each individual presents their concepts to the group.
13. In larger groups each group of 4 can select 3 favored ideas in smaller group to present to larger group. Each smaller group selects a presenter.
14. Moderator and group can evaluate the concepts using a list of heuristics.
15. Put all the sketches or post it notes on a wall.
16. Group concepts into categories of related ideas.
17. Dot vote each category to determine best ideas to carry forward.
18. Do another round of sketching focusing of 3 best ideas.
19. Iterate this process as many times as necessary.
20. Record session with digital images.
21. Smaller group can take preferred ideas and develop them after the session.

RESOURCES

1. Large space
2. Tables
3. Chairs
4. White boards
5. Dry-erase markers
6. Camera
7. Post-it-notes
8. Materials such as cardboard, children's construction kits

0.5 day ux charette

HOW TO USE THIS METHOD

1. Choose a problem to focus on.
2. Select moderator.
3. Select and invite participants.
4. Team size of 4 to 20 participants preferred representing users, managers, design and diverse group of stakeholders.
5. Break down teams over 8 into smaller groups of 4 or 5 participants.
6. Brief participants in advance by email.
7. Allow one hour per problem
8. Use creative space such as a room with a large table and whiteboard.
9. Brief participants allow 15 minutes to one hour for individual concept exploration.
10. Give participants a goal such as 5 concepts.
11. Output can be wireframes or storyboards.
12. Each individual presents their concepts to the group.
13. Moderator and group can evaluate the concepts using a list of heuristics.
14. Put all the sketches or post it notes on a wall.
15. Group concepts into categories of related ideas.
16. Dot vote each category to determine best ideas to carry forward.
17. Do another round of sketching focusing of 3 best ideas.
18. Iterate this process as many times as necessary.
19. Record session with digital images.
20. Smaller group can take preferred ideas and develop them after the session.

RESOURCES

1. Large space
2. Tables
3. Chairs
4. White boards
5. Dry-erase markers
6. Camera
7. Post-it-notes

1.5 day mini charette

HOW TO USE THIS METHOD

Day 1

1. Evening mixer night before event.
2. Breakfast 30 minutes.
3. Moderator introduces participants expectations and goals.
4. Overview of project 30 mins
5. Break 15 minutes
6. Individual presenters present information about aspects of project 1 hour
7. Lunch 1 hour
8. Further presentations related to aspects of project 1 hour
9. Question and answer session 15 minutes
10. Multi disciplinary breakout groups 2.5 hours
11. Group size preferred 4 to 8 participants.
12. Groups explore strategies and issues.
13. Groups present strategies and goals to larger group 30 minutes. Larger group brainstorms goals.
14. Site tour 1 hour - for urban or architectural projects.

Day 2

1. Breakfast 30 minutes
2. Review of Day 1, 30 minutes.
3. Breakout groups explore concept solutions as sketches 2.5 hours.
4. Groups present to larger group 30 minutes.
5. Larger group brainstorms next steps 30 minutes
6. Lunch 1 hour

RESOURCES

1. Large space
2. Tables
3. Chairs
4. White boards
5. Dry-erase markers
6. Camera
7. Post-it-notes

2.0 day design charette

HOW TO USE THIS METHOD

Day 1
1. Evening mixer night before event.
2. Breakfast 30 minutes.
3. Moderator introduces participants expectations and goals.
4. Overview of project 30 mins
5. Break 15 minutes
6. Individual presenters present information about aspects of project 1 hour
7. Lunch 1 hour
8. Further presentations related to aspects of project 1 hour
9. Question and answer session 15 minutes
10. Multi disciplinary breakout groups 2.5 hours
11. Group size preferred 4 to 8 participants.
12. Groups explore strategies and issues.
13. Groups present strategies and goals to larger group 30 minutes. Larger group brainstorms goals.
14. Site tour 1 hour – for urban or architectural projects.

Day 2
1. Breakfast 30 minutes
2. Review of Day 1, 30 minutes.
3. Breakout groups explore concept solutions as sketches 2.5 hours.
4. Groups present to larger group 30 minutes.
5. Lunch 1 hour
6. Breakout groups refine concept solutions as sketches 2.5 hours.
7. Groups present to larger group 30 minutes.
8. Wrap up and next steps 30 minutes

RESOURCES
1. Large space
2. Tables
3. Chairs
4. White boards
5. Dry-erase markers
6. Camera
7. Post-it-notes

4.0 day architectural charette

HOW TO USE THIS METHOD
1. Define problem
2. Public meeting Vision
3. Brief group
4. Alternative concepts generated
5. Small groups work
6. Small groups present.
7. Whole group discussion
8. Public meeting input
9. Preferred concepts developed
10. Small groups work
11. Small groups present.
12. Whole group discussion
13. Open house review
14. Small groups work
15. Small groups present.
16. Whole group discussion
17. Further plan development.
18. Public meeting confirmation of final design.

RESOURCES
1. Large space
2. Tables
3. Chairs
4. White boards
5. Dry-erase markers
6. Camera
7. Post-it-notes

635 method design charette

HOW TO USE THIS METHOD
1. Choose a problem to focus on.
2. Select moderator.
3. Select and invite participants.
4. Team size of 4 to 20 participants preferred representing users, managers, design and diverse group of stakeholders.
5. Break down teams into groups of 3 participants.
6. Each group of 3 should sit at a separate table.
7. Brief participants in advance by e-mail.
8. Allow one hour per problem
9. Use creative space such as a room with a large table and whiteboard.
10. Brief participants allow 15 minutes to one hour for individual concept exploration.
11. Can use egg timer to time sessions.
12. Give each participant a goal such as 5 concepts.
13. At end of concept exploration time group selects the best 3 concepts from the session and two participants move to another table. One participant stays at table.
14. The session is repeated each group combines the best ideas from two tables.
15. Repeat this process five times.
16. At the end of these concept exploration session pin all the drawings on a wall and group by affinities.
17. Moderator and group can evaluate the concepts using a list of heuristics.
18. Dot vote each category to determine best ideas to carry forward.
19. Do another round of sketching focusing of 3 best ideas.
20. Record session with digital images.
21. Smaller group can take preferred ideas and develop them after the session.

RESOURCES
1. Large space
2. Tables
3. Chairs
4. White boards
5. Dry-erase markers
6. Camera
7. Post-it-notes

desirability testing

WHAT IS IT?

Desirability testing are a number of qualitative and quantitative attitudinal methods that assess people's attitudes to a product or service.

WHY USE THIS METHOD?

1. A manager often feels his or her perception of a design is just as valid as the designer's
2. These methods help the design team understand the response of customers to a proposed design.
3. Reduces the subjectivity of design decisions.

CHALLENGES

1. This method measures attitude rather than behavior.

WHEN TO USE THIS METHOD

1. Define intent
2. Know Context and user
3. Frame insights
4. Explore Concepts

HOW TO USE THIS METHOD

1. Participants are given cards that have words on each card such as desirable, high quality, valuable, useful, reliable, fun confusing, complex, familiar.
2. The participants select the cards that go with each design.
3. The researcher asks the participants why they made the selections.

RESOURCES

1. Word cards
2. Table
3. Prototype products or services

digital ethnography

WHAT IS IT?

Digital Ethnography is research that is undertaken in online, virtual or digitally enabled environments. It uses digital tools to gather, analyze, and present ethnographic data.

WHY USE THIS METHOD?

1. Can be faster and less expensive than non-digital methods.
2. Data collected real time
3. Access to people may be easier
4. People carry digital devices such as smart phones, cameras, laptops and tablets
5. Data can be gathered in context

CHALLENGES

1. Can miss non verbal feedback.
2. Technology may be unreliable

WHEN TO USE THIS METHOD

1. Define intent
2. Know Context
3. Know User
4. Frame insights
5. Explore Concepts
6. Make Plans
7. Deliver Offering

HOW TO USE THIS METHOD

There are many different methods which use or access:

1. Audio conferences
2. Web conferences
3. Virtual in depth interviews
4. Focus groups
5. Mobile diaries
6. Online forums
7. Private online communities

RESOURCES

1. Smart phones,
2. Cameras,
3. Laptops and
4. Tablets

REFERENCES

1. Coover, R. (2004) 'Using Digital Media Tools and Cross-Cultural Research,Analysis and Representation', Visual Studies19(1): 6—25.
2. Dicks, B., B. Mason, A. Coffey and P. Atkinson (2005) Qualitative Research and Hypermedia: Ethnography for the Digital Age. London: SAGE.
3. Kozinets R.V. (2010a), Netnography. Doing Ethnographic Research Online, Sage, London.

dramaturgy

WHAT IS IT?
Dramaturgy is a method that uses drama techniques to help understand user behaviors and needs. It a form of prototyping.

WHO INVENTED IT?
Robert, Benford D., and Scott A. Hunt

WHY USE THIS METHOD?
1. Created to make personas more dynamic.

CHALLENGES
1. Some team members may be uncomfortable with drama based activity.
2. The method is not in context
3. The method may be subjective as it does not involve the people being designed for,

WHEN TO USE THIS METHOD
4. Know Context
5. Know User
6. Frame insights
7. Explore Concepts

HOW TO USE THIS METHOD
1. Choose a character
2. Create groups of 2 or 3 members of your design team
3. Ask your teams to write monologues for the characters based on public, private and intimate levels.
4. Ask your team to discuss the rituals of the character's lives
5. Ask your team to create maps of the stakeholders
6. Create scenes exploring crucial moments in your character's experiences or interactions.
7. Present these scenarios with groups of actors.
8. Explore the problems and challenges of the character's experiences and interactions.

REFERENCES
1. Robert, Benford D., and Scott A. Hunt. "Dramaturgy and Social Movements: The Social Construction and Communication of Power." Social Inquiry 62.1 (2007): 36-55. Wiley Online Library.

drawing experiences

WHAT IS IT?

This method involves asking respondents to create drawings to illustrate their experiences.

WHO INVENTED IT?

Used by design consultants IDEO

WHY USE THIS METHOD?

1. Drawing can elicit information difficult for respondents to describe in words.

CHALLENGES

1. A drawing of an experience is different to an experience which involves all senses.
2. Some people are not confident expressing themselves through drawing.

WHEN TO USE THIS METHOD

1. Know Context
2. Know User
3. Frame insights

HOW TO USE THIS METHOD

1. Select a moderator
2. Select a group of 4 to 12 users
3. Ask users to create an image of an experience through a drawing.

RESOURCES

1. Pens
2. Paper

REFERENCES

1. IDEO method cards. Publication Date: November 2003 ISBN-10: 0954413210 ISBN-13: 978-0954413217

ACTIVITY PHASE | ACTIVITY PHASE | ACTIVITY PHASE | ACTIVITY PHASE | ACTIVITY PHASE

emotional journey map

WHAT IS IT?
An emotional journey map is a map that visually illustrates people's emotional experience throughout an interaction with an organization or brand.

WHY USE THIS METHOD?
1. It provides a focus for discussion
2. It focusses on what may make your customers unhappy
3. Provides a visually compelling story of customer experience.
4. Customer experience is more than interaction with a product.
5. By understanding the journey that your customers are making, you will be in a position to make informed improvements.

CHALLENGES
1. Customers often do not take the route in an interaction that the designer expects.
2. Failure to manage experiences can lead to lost customers.

WHEN TO USE THIS METHOD
1. Know Context
2. Know User
3. Frame insights
4. Explore Concepts
5. Make Plans

HOW TO USE THIS METHOD
1. Define the activity of your map. For example it could be a ride on the underground train.
2. Collect internal insights
3. Research customer perceptions
4. Analyze research
5. Map journey.
6. Across the top of the page do a time line Break the journey into stages using your customer's point of view
7. Capture each persona's unique experience
8. Use a scale from 0 to 10. The higher the number, the better the experience.
9. Plot the emotional journey.
10. Analyze the lease pleasant emotional periods and create ideas for improving the experience during those periods.
11. Create a map for each persona.

RESOURCES
1. Paper
2. Pens
3. White board
4. Post-it-notes

REFERENCES
1. Joshi, Hetal. "Customer Journey Mapping: The Road to Success." Cognizant. (2009) Web. 26 Jul. 2013.
2. World Class Skills Programme. "Customer Journey Mapping." Developing Responsive Provision. (2006): n. page. Web. 27 Jul. 2013.

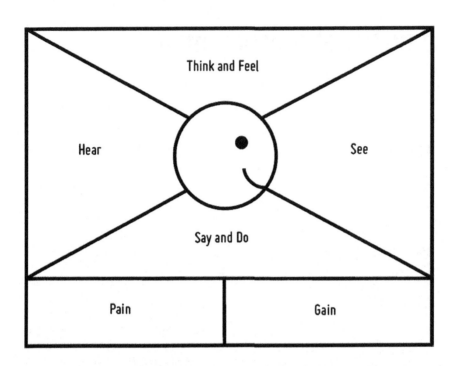

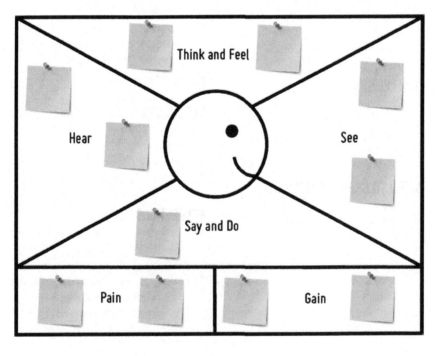

empathy map

WHAT IS IT?
Empathy Map is a tool that helps the design team empathize with people they are designing for, You can create an empathy map for a group of customers or a persona.

WHO INVENTED IT?
Scott Matthews and Dave Gray at PLANE now Dachis Group.

WHY USE THIS METHOD?
This tool helps a design team understand the customers and their context.

CHALLENGES
1. Emotions must be inferred by observing clues.
2. This method does not provide the same level of rigor as traditional personas but requires less investment.

WHEN TO USE THIS METHOD
1. Know Context
2. Know User
3. Frame insights

RESOURCES
1. Empathy map template
2. White board
3. Dry-erase markers
4. Post-it-notes
5. Pens
6. Video Camera

HOW TO USE THIS METHOD
1. A team of 3 to 10 people is a good number for this method.
2. This method can be used with personas.
3. Draw a cirle to represent your target persona.
4. Divide the circle into sections that represent aspects of that person's sensory experience.
5. Ask your team to describe from the persona's point of view their experience.
6. What are the persona's needs and desires?
7. Populate the map by taking note of the following traits of your user as you review your notes, audio, and video from your fieldwork: What are they thinking, feeling, saying, doing, hearing, seeing?
8. Fill in the diagram with real, tangible, sensory experiences.
9. 20 minutes to one hour is a good duration for this exercise.
10. Ask another group of people to look at your map and suggest improvements or refinements.

REFERENCES
1. Gray, Dave; Brown, Sunni; Macanufo, James (2010). Gamestorming: A Playbook for Innovators, Rulebreakers, and Changemakers. O'Reilly Media, Inc

empathy probes

WHAT IS IT?
This method involves participants recording specific events, feelings or interactions, in a diary supplied by the researcher. User Diaries help provide insight into behavior. Participants record their behavior and thoughts. Diaries can uncover behavior that may not be articulated in an interview or easily visible to outsiders.

WHO INVENTED IT?
Gordon Allport, may have been the first to describe diary studies in 1942.

WHY USE THIS METHOD?
1. Can capture data that is difficult to capture using other methods.
2. Cultural probes are appropriate when you need to gather information from users with minimal influence on their actions,
3. When the process or event you're exploring takes place intermittently or
4. When the process or event you're exploring takes place over a long period.

CHALLENGES
1. Process can be expensive and time consuming.
2. Needs participant monitoring.
3. Diary can fit into users' pocket.
4. It is difficult to get materials back.

WHEN TO USE THIS METHOD
1. Know Context
2. Know User
3. Frame insights

HOW TO USE THIS METHOD
1. A diary can be kept over a period of one week or longer.
2. Define focus for the study.
3. Recruit participants carefully.
4. Decide method: preprinted, diary notebook or online.
5. Prepare diary packs. Can be preprinted sheets or blank 20 page notebooks with prepared questions or online web based diary.
6. Brief participants.
7. Distribute diaries directly or by mail.
8. Conduct study. Keep in touch with participants.
9. Conduct debrief interview.
10. Look for insights.

RESOURCES
1. Diary
2. Preprinted diary sheets
3. Online diary
4. Pens
5. Disposable cameras
6. Digital camera
7. Self addressed envelopes

REFERENCES
1. Bailey, Kathleen M. (1990) The use of diary studies in teacher education programs In Richards, J. C. & Nunan, D. (org.). Second Language Teacher Education (pp. 215–226). Cambridge: Cambridge University Press.

SEE ALSO
Diary study

empathy tools

WHAT IS IT?

Empathy tools are aids or tools that help designers empathize with the people they are designing for. They can be used to test a prototype design or in activities such as role playing or body storming.

WHO INVENTED IT?

Brandt, E. and Grunnet, C 2000

WHY USE THIS METHOD?

1. To help a designer understand the experiences of people that they are designing for.

CHALLENGES

1. Empathy tools are imperfect approximations of user experiences.

WHEN TO USE THIS METHOD

1. Know Context
2. Know User
3. Frame insights
4. Explore Concept

HOW TO USE THIS METHOD

1. Wear heavy gloves to experience less sensitivity in your hands
2. Wear fogged glasses to experience less acute vision
3. Wear black glasses to eat to experience issues locating food and utensils.
4. Spend a day in a wheelchair.
5. Wear earplugs to experience diminished hearing

RESOURCES

1. Wheelchair
2. Fogged glasses
3. Blackened glasses
4. Gloves
5. Earplugs
6. Crutches
7. Walking stick

REFERENCES

1. Brandt, E. and Grunnet, C., "Evoking the Future: Drama and Props in User-centered Design", PDC 2000

ethnocentrism

WHAT IS IT?

Ethnocentrism is a characteristic of human behavior that can stand in the way of creating effective design solutions. As designers are working increasingly on global projects ethnocentrism is becoming something which needs to be more carefully considered. Ethnocentrism is judging another culture only by the values and standards of one's own culture. Ethnocentrism leads to misunderstanding others. We falsely distort what is meaningful and functional to other peoples through our own tinted glasses

WHO INVENTED IT?

William G. Sumner first used the term

WHY USE THIS METHOD?

1. Ethnocentrism can lead to failed design efforts.
2. Ethnocentrism can lead to conflicts.

CHALLENGES

1. It is useful to recognize ethnocentrism when designing across cultures and to make efforts to reduce it's impact on the outcomes of a project.

Image Copyright Warren Goldswain 2013 Used under license from Shutterstock.com

WHEN TO USE THIS METHOD

1. Define intent
2. Know Context
3. Know User
4. Frame insights
5. Explore Concepts

TO REDUCE ETHNOCENTRISM

1. Recognize that we do not understand, that we are falsely assuming something that is not the case and is out of context.
2. Control our biases and to seek more valid and balanced understanding.
3. Ask "How are the behaviors meaningful and functional to the people being studied?"
4. When we encounter ethnocentrism being promoted by particular groups, we can ask ourselves and those around us "Why are they doing this?" What function does promoting ethnocentrism

REFERENCES

1. Ankerl, G. Coexisting Contemporary Civilizations: Arabo-Muslim, Bharati, Chinese, and Western. Geneva: INU PRESS, 2000, ISBN 2-88155-004-5
2. Reynolds, V., Falger, V., & Vine, I. (Eds.) (1987). The Sociobiology of Ethnocentrism. Athens, GA: University of Georgia Press.
3. Shimp, Terence. Sharma, Shubhash. "Consumer Ethnocentrism: Construction and Validation of the CETSCALE. Journal of Marketing Research. 24 (3). Aug 1987.

EVALUATION MATRIX

CRITERIA	WEIGHT	DESIGN A		DESIGN B		DESIGN C		DESIGN D	
		SCORE	WEIGHTED	SCORE	WEIGHTED	SCORE	WEIGHTED	SCORE	WEIGHTED
TOTAL									

evaluation matrix

WHAT IS IT?

A simple tool used for planning and conducting an evaluation that aids the team in making informed decisions by comparing many options. The use of an evaluation matrix is a method of evaluating a number of options against a number of criteria. A Weighted Alternatives Evaluation Matrix, or Weighted Matrix, assigns weighting factors to criteria when comparing alternatives

WHY USE THIS METHOD?

1. Control costs by focusing resources
2. Answer/discover critical questions.
3. Fast and cost effective method.
4. Allows you to identify strengths and weaknesses.
5. An efficient way of conveying information.

CHALLENGES

1. Can emphasize data which is not most important.
2. Assignment of weights and scores is subjective

WHEN TO USE THIS METHOD

1. Know Context
2. Know User
3. Frame insights
4. Explore Concepts
5. Make Plans

HOW TO USE THIS METHOD

1. Establishing Evaluation Criteria.
2. Prioritizing criteria
3. List mandatory criteria
4. List desirable criteria
5. The simplest Alternatives Evaluation Matrix indicates with a yes or no whether each criterion was met.
6. Weighting factors are used to define the level of importance of criteria. Assigning meaning to weighting factors is subjective. Keep the number of weighting factors small
7. You can have the members of a group do their own ranking and then combine the results onto one summary report.
8. Analyze the criteria rankings

RESOURCES

1. Paper
2. Pens
3. White board
4. Dry-erase markers

explore represent share

WHAT IS IT?
This is a process for designing your own user research methods. It is a structured group facilitation process.

WHO INVENTED IT?
Denis O'Brien

WHEN TO USE THIS METHOD
1. Explore Concepts

HOW TO USE THIS METHOD
1. Participants are encouraged to explore ideas, represent them in words, drawings and objects and share their meanings.
2. The moderator prompts respondents with written questions to document their thoughts on paper.
3. Some sample prompts are:
"My ideal research method would be."
"This wouldn't work because."
4. Participants interpret each others output.
5. When we encounter ethnocentrism being promoted by particular groups, we can ask ourselves and those around us "Why are they doing this?" What function does promoting ethnocentrism

RESOURCES
1. Pens
2. Paper
3. Video camera
4. Digital voice recorder
5. Forms

REFERENCES
1. O'Brien, Denis. The Methods Lab: Explore, Represent, Share.
2. Koberg, Don, Bagnall, Jim. The Universal Traveler: a Soft-Systems guide to creativity, problem-solving, and the process of reaching goals.
3. J. Christopher Jones, Design Methods (New York: Van Nostrand Reinhold, 1992).

eyetracking

WHAT IS IT?

Eye tracking is a group of methods of studying and recording a person's eye movements over time. The most widely used current designs are video-based eye trackers. One of the most prominent fields of commercial eye tracking research is web usability but this method is also used widely for evaluating retail interiors and products.

WHO INVENTED IT?

Louis Émile Javal 1879
Alfred L. Yarbus 1950s

WHY USE THIS METHOD?

1. Examine which details attract attention.
2. To record where a participant's attention is focussed for example on a supermarket shelf which products and parts of products attract the most attention from shoppers.

CHALLENGES

1. Each method of eye tracking has advantages and disadvantages, and the choice of an eye tracking system depends on considerations of cost and application.
2. A poorly adjusted system can produce unreliable information.

WHEN TO USE THIS METHOD

1. Know Context
2. Know User
3. Frame insights
4. Explore Concepts

TYPES OF SYSTEMS

1. Measures eye movement with a device attached to the eye. For example a contact lens with a magnetic field sensor.
2. Non contact measurement of eye movement. For example infrared, is reflected from the eye and sensed by a video camera.
3. Measures eye movement with electrodes placed around the eyes.

TYPES OF OUTPUTS

1. Heat maps
2. Gaze plots
3. Gaze replays

RESOURCES

1. Eye tracking device
2. Software
3. Laptop computer

REFERENCES

1. Bojko, A. (2006). Using Eye Tracking to Compare Web Page Designs: A Case Study. Journal of Usability Studies, Vol.1, No. 3.
2. Chandon, Pierre, J. Wesley Hutchinson, and Scott H. Young (2001), Measuring Value of Point-of-Purchase Marketing with Commercial Eye-Tracking Data.
3. Wedel, M. & Pieters, R. (2000). Eye fixations on advertisements and memory for brands: a model and findings. Marketing Science, 19 (4), 2000, 297–312.

field study

WHAT IS IT?

A field study is a study carried on in the context of people rather than in design studio or a laboratory. A field study is primary research It involves observing or interviewing people in their natural environments.

WHO INVENTED IT?

James Cowles Prichard 1841
Margaret Mead, 1928
Bronisław Malinowski, 1929
Pierre Bourdieu 1958-1962

WHY USE THIS METHOD?

1. A field study can be used to inform design and to create more successful outcomes for design by better informing the designer of the behaviors, desires and needs of the people being designed for.

CHALLENGES

1. May be more expensive than secondary research.
2. Information may become obsolete

WHEN TO USE THIS METHOD

1. Define intent
2. Know Context
3. Know User
4. Frame insights
5. Explore Concepts
6. Make Plans
7. Deliver Offering

HOW TO USE THIS METHOD

1. Define goals.
2. Develop plan
3. Create study materials such as question guides, release forms,
4. Prepare for site visits
5. Perform observations and interviews.
6. Analyze data
7. Develop insights
8. Make recommendations.

RESOURCES

1. Note pads
2. Pens
3. Digital camera
4. Video camera
5. Post-it notes

REFERENCES

1. Jarvie, I. C. (1967) On Theories of Fieldwork and the Scientific Character of Social Anthropology, Philosophy of Science, Vol. 34, No. 3 (Sep., 1967), pp. 223-242.
2. Marek M. Kaminski. 2004. Games Prisoners Play. Princeton University Press. ISBN 0-691-11721-7

field experiment

WHAT IS IT?

A field experiment is an experiment conducted outside the laboratory, in a 'natural' context This method often involves changing one or more variables in a context to understand their effect and randomizing participants into treatment and control groups.

WHO INVENTED IT?

Abu Rayman al-Biruni 1030 AD

WHY USE THIS METHOD?

1. Because the settings are more natural it is assumed that people will behave more naturally
2. Less sample bias.
3. Fewer demand characteristics if participants are unaware.
4. Designers conduct field experiments with prototypes to obtain feedback and refine designs.

CHALLENGES

1. Difficult to replicate
2. Informed consent may be difficult to obtain.
3. Less control of variables
4. Difficult to replicate.
5. Difficult to record data accurately.
6. If participants are unaware of the study how can the consent to take part or withdraw from the experiment?
7. Many participants are required to make reliable claims

WHEN TO USE THIS METHOD

1. Know Context
2. Know User
3. Frame insights

HOW TO USE THIS METHOD

Various methods are possible
Consider:

1. What resources are available
2. What will you test and compare?
3. What will be your methods?
4. How will you gain access and participation?

RESOURCES

1. Note pad
2. Pens
3. Camera
4. Video camera
5. Digital voice recorder

REFERENCES

1. Reichardt, C. S. & Mark, M. M. (2004). Quasi-Experimentation. In J. S. Wholey, H. P. Hatry, & K. E. Newcomber (Eds.) Handbook of Practical Program Evaluation, Second Edition, San Franciso: Jossey-Bass.

fly-on-the-wall

WHAT IS IT?

Observation method where the observer remains as unobtrusive as possible and observes and collects data relevant to a research study in context with no interaction with the participants being observed. The name derived from the documentary film technique of the same name.

WHO INVENTED IT?

ALex Bavelas 1944
Lucy Vernile, Robert A. Monteiro 1991

WHY USE THIS METHOD?

1. Low cost
2. No setup necessary
3. Can observe a large number of participants.
4. Objective observations
5. Compared to other methods such as focus groups, setup, data collection, and processing are much faster.

CHALLENGES

1. No interaction by the observer.
2. Requires that the observer be silent during the presentation without asking questions or making suggestions.
3. Observer cannot delve deeper during a session.
4. No interruption allowed
5. Observer cannot obtain details on customer comments during a session

Photo: photocase.com - FreyaSapphire

WHEN TO USE THIS METHOD

1. Know Context
2. Know User
3. Frame insights

HOW TO USE THIS METHOD

1. Define activity to study
2. Select participants thoughtfully
3. Choose a context for the observation
4. Carefully observe the interaction or experience. This is best done by members of your design team.
5. It is important to influence the participants as little as possible by your presence.
6. Observe but do not interact with participants while observing them in context.
7. Capture Data
8. Identify issues
9. Identify needs
10. Create design solutions based on observed and experienced human needs.

RESOURCES

1. Digital camera
2. Video camera
3. Notebook
4. Pens
5. Voice recorder

REFERENCES

1. McDonald, Seonaidh. "Studying Actions in Context: A Qualitative Shadowing Method for Organizational Research." Qualitative Research. The Robert Gordon University. SAGE Publications. London. 2005. p455-473.

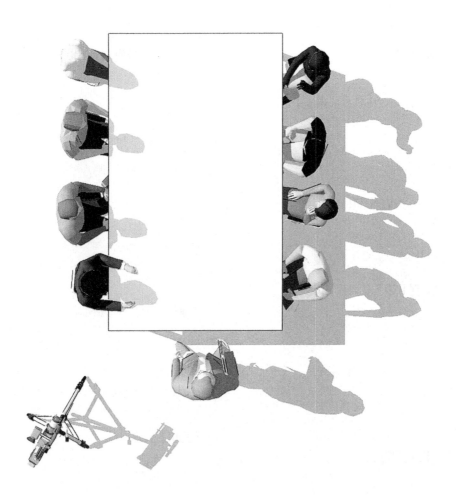

focus groups

WHAT IS IT?

Focus groups are discussions usually with 6 to 12 participants led by a moderator. Focus groups are used during the the design of products, services and experiences to get feedback from people

Powell defined a focus group as "A group of individuals selected and assembled by researchers to discuss and comment on, from personal experience, the topic that is the subject of the research."

WHO INVENTED IT?

Robert K. Merton 1940 Bureau of Applied Social Research.

WHY USE THIS METHOD?

1. To identify the expectations, needs and desires of customers.
2. It is useful to gain several different perspectives about a design problem.
3. A disadvantage of this method is that it removes the subjects from their context.

CHALLENGES

1. Focus group study results may not be not be generalizable.
2. Focus group participants can influence each other.

WHEN TO USE THIS METHOD

1. Know Context
2. Know User
3. Frame insights
4. Explore Concepts

HOW TO USE THIS METHOD

1. Select a good moderator.
2. Prepare a screening questionnaire.
3. Decide incentives for participants.
4. Select facility.
5. Recruit participants. Invite participants to your session well in advance and get firm commitments to attend. Remind participants the date of the event.
6. Participants should sit around a large table. Follow discussion guide.
7. Describe rules. Provide refreshments.
8. First question should encourage talking and participation.
9. The moderator manages responses and asks important questions
10. Moderator collects forms and debriefs focus group.
11. Analyze results while still fresh.
12. Summarize key points.
13. Run additional focus groups to deepen analysis.

RESOURCES

1. Focus group space.
2. Sound and video recording equipment
3. White board
4. Pens
5. Post-it-notes

REFERENCES

1. Nachmais, Chava Frankfort; Nachmais, David. 2008. Research methods in the Social Sciences: Seventh Edition New York, NY: Worth Publishers

focus group: client participant

WHAT IS IT?
A client participant focus group allows the client to participate either visibly or invisibly through a one way mirror. This method allows the client to interpret the answers and the a participant's body language and to ensure that the discussion covers what the client would like to be covered.

WHO INVENTED IT?
Robert K. Merton 1940 Bureau of Applied Social Research.

WHY USE THIS METHOD?
1. A focus group allows an in depth probe.
2. Interaction between participants can uncover broader insights.
3. They are cost effective for the volume and quality of data
4. Are less expensive than conducting 8 to 12 in depth interviews
5. Are time efficient
6. Clients can gain insights by observing the group interaction through a one way mirror.

CHALLENGES
1. Participants can influence each other.
2. Data is not quantifiable.
3. Responses are limited.
4. Data may be difficult to analyze
5. The participants are out of the context of their usual environments.

WHEN TO USE THIS METHOD
1. Know Context
2. Know User
3. Frame insights
4. Explore Concepts

HOW TO USE THIS METHOD
1. Focus groups often take one and a half to two hours.
2. Ask 5 to 10 questions.
3. Define purpose
4. Ask:
   ◦ Why a focus group?
   ◦ Who are the stakeholders?
   ◦ Who is the target population?
   ◦ What problems will be explored?
5. Define resources
6. Write question guide.
7. Recruit participants.
8. Conduct focus group.
9. Analyze data.
10. Create insights.
11. Take actions.

RESOURCES
1. Focus group space.
2. Sound and video recording equipment
3. White board
4. Pens
5. Post-it-notes

REFERENCES
1. Nachmais, Chava Frankfort; Nachmais, David. 2008. Research methods in the Social Sciences: Seventh Edition New York, NY: Worth Publishers

focus group: devil's advocate

WHAT IS IT?
This with method two moderators present contrary viewpoints. The different ways of thinking provide new insights.

WHO INVENTED IT?
Robert K. Merton 1940 Bureau of Applied Social Research.

WHY USE THIS METHOD?
1. A focus group allows an in depth probe.
2. Interaction between participants can uncover broader insights.
3. They are cost effective for the volume and quality of data
4. Are less expensive than conducting 8 to 12 in depth interviews
5. Are time efficient
6. Clients can gain insights by observing the group interaction through a one way mirror.

CHALLENGES
1. Participants can influence each other.
2. Data is not quantifiable.
3. Responses are limited.
4. Data may be difficult to analyze
5. The participants are out of the context of their usual environments.

WHEN TO USE THIS METHOD
1. Know Context
2. Know User
3. Frame insights
4. Explore Concepts

HOW TO USE THIS METHOD
1. Focus groups often take one and a half to two hours.
2. Ask 5 to 10 questions.
3. Define purpose
4. Ask:
   ◦ Why a focus group?
   ◦ Who are the stakeholders?
   ◦ Who is the target population?
   ◦ What problems will be explored?
5. Define resources
6. Write question guide.
7. Recruit participants.
8. Conduct focus group.
9. Analyze data.
10. Create insights.
11. Take actions.

RESOURCES
1. Focus group space.
2. Sound and video recording equipment
3. White board
4. Pens
5. Post-it-notes

REFERENCES
1. Nachmais, Chava Frankfort; Nachmais, David. 2008. Research methods in the Social Sciences: Seventh Edition New York, NY: Worth Publishers

focus group: dual moderator

WHAT IS IT?

The dual moderator focus group involves two moderators. One moderator manages the time progression. The second moderator ensures that the discussion remains on the focus topics.

WHO INVENTED IT?

Robert K. Merton 1940 Bureau of Applied Social Research.

WHY USE THIS METHOD?

1. A focus group allows an in depth probe.
2. Interaction between participants can uncover broader insights.
3. They are cost effective for the volume and quality of data
4. Are less expensive than conducting 8 to 12 in depth interviews
5. Are time efficient
6. Clients can gain insights by observing the group interaction through a one way mirror.

CHALLENGES

1. Participants can influence each other.
2. Data is not quantifiable.
3. Responses are limited.
4. Data may be difficult to analyze
5. The participants are out of the context of their usual environments.

WHEN TO USE THIS METHOD

1. Know Context
2. Know User
3. Frame insights
4. Explore Concepts

HOW TO USE THIS METHOD

1. Focus groups often take one and a half to two hours.
2. Ask 5 to 10 questions.
3. Define purpose
4. Ask:
    - Why a focus group?
    - Who are the stakeholders?
    - Who is the target population?
    - What problems will be explored?
5. Define resources
6. Write question guide.
7. Recruit participants.
8. Conduct focus group.
9. Analyze data.
10. Create insights.
11. Take actions.

RESOURCES

1. Focus group space.
2. Sound and video recording equipment
3. White board
4. Pens
5. Post-it-notes

REFERENCES

1. Nachmais, Chava Frankfort; Nachmais, David. 2008. Research methods in the Social Sciences: Seventh Edition New York, NY: Worth Publishers

focus group: mini focus group

WHAT IS IT?

A mini focus group has four or five participants. Other methods commonly involve eight to twelve participants. This method may be appropriate for exploring more intimate or sensitive subjects.

WHO INVENTED IT?

Robert K. Merton 1940 Bureau of Applied Social Research.

WHY USE THIS METHOD?

1. A focus group allows an in depth probe.
2. Interaction between participants can uncover broader insights.
3. They are cost effective for the volume and quality of data
4. Are less expensive than conducting 8 to 12 in depth interviews
5. Are time efficient
6. Clients can gain insights by observing the group interaction through a one way mirror.

CHALLENGES

1. Participants can influence each other.
2. Data is not quantifiable.
3. Responses are limited.
4. Data may be difficult to analyze
5. The participants are out of the context of their usual environments.

WHEN TO USE THIS METHOD

1. Know Context
2. Know User
3. Frame insights
4. Explore Concepts

HOW TO USE THIS METHOD

1. Focus groups often take one and a half to two hours.
2. Ask 5 to 10 questions.
3. Define purpose
4. Ask:
   ◦ Why a focus group?
   ◦ Who are the stakeholders?
   ◦ Who is the target population?
   ◦ What problems will be explored?
5. Define resources
6. Write question guide.
7. Recruit participants.
8. Conduct focus group.
9. Analyze data.
10. Create insights.
11. Take actions.

RESOURCES

1. Focus group space.
2. Sound and video recording equipment
3. White board
4. Pens
5. Post-it-notes

REFERENCES

1. Nachmais, Chava Frankfort; Nachmais, David. 2008. Research methods in the Social Sciences: Seventh Edition New York, NY: Worth Publishers

focus group: online

WHAT IS IT?
This is a focus group where the participants are involved from different locations via their computers.

WHO INVENTED IT?
Robert K. Merton 1940 Bureau of Applied Social Research.

WHY USE THIS METHOD?
1. A focus group allows an in depth probe.
2. Interaction between participants can uncover broader insights.
3. They are cost effective for the volume and quality of data
4. Are less expensive than conducting 8 to 12 in depth interviews
5. Are time efficient
6. Clients can gain insights by observing the group interaction through a one way mirror.

CHALLENGES
1. Participants can influence each other.
2. Data is not quantifiable.
3. Responses are limited.
4. Data may be difficult to analyze
5. The participants are out of the context of their usual environments.

WHEN TO USE THIS METHOD
1. Know Context
2. Know User
3. Frame insights
4. Explore Concepts

HOW TO USE THIS METHOD
1. Define purpose
2. Ask:
- Why a focus group?
- Who are the stakeholders?
- Who is the target population?
- What problems will be explored?
3. Define resources
4. Write question guide.
5. Recruit participants.
6. Conduct focus group.
7. Analyze data.
8. Create insights.
9. Take actions.

RESOURCES
1. Focus group space.
2. Sound and video recording equipment
3. White board
4. Pens
5. Post-it-notes

REFERENCES
1. Nachmais, Chava Frankfort; Nachmais, David. 2008. Research methods in the Social Sciences: Seventh Edition New York, NY: Worth Publishers

focus group: other participant

WHAT IS IT?
One or more selected people participate as a group member or moderator in the discussion temporarily or for the full duration. This may be an expert such as the designer, writer, or some other specialist.

WHO INVENTED IT?
Robert K. Merton 1940 Bureau of Applied Social Research.

WHY USE THIS METHOD?
1. A focus group allows an in depth probe.
2. Interaction between participants can uncover broader insights.
3. They are cost effective for the volume and quality of data
4. Are less expensive than conducting 8 to 12 in depth interviews
5. Are time efficient
6. Clients can gain insights by observing the group interaction through a one way mirror.

CHALLENGES
1. Participants can influence each other.
2. Data is not quantifiable.
3. Responses are limited.
4. Data may be difficult to analyze
5. The participants are out of the context of their usual environments.

WHEN TO USE THIS METHOD
1. Know Context
2. Know User
3. Frame insights
4. Explore Concepts

HOW TO USE THIS METHOD
1. Focus groups often take one and a half to two hours.
2. Ask:
   ◦ Why a focus group?
   ◦ Who are the stakeholders?
   ◦ Who is the target population?
   ◦ What problems will be explored?
3. Define resources
4. Write question guide.
5. Recruit participants.
6. Conduct focus group.
7. Analyze data.
8. Create insights.
9. Take actions.

RESOURCES
1. Focus group space.
2. Sound and video recording equipment
3. White board
4. Pens
5. Post-it-notes

REFERENCES
1. Nachmais, Chava Frankfort; Nachmais, David. 2008. Research methods in the Social Sciences: Seventh Edition New York, NY: Worth Publishers

focus group:
respondent moderator

WHAT IS IT?

A respondent moderator focus group involves the participants and moderator exchanging roles. A diversity of viewpoints from a number of different moderators results in more honest diverse responses

WHO INVENTED IT?

Robert K. Merton 1940 Bureau of Applied Social Research.

WHY USE THIS METHOD?

1. A focus group allows an in depth probe.
2. Interaction between participants can uncover broader insights.
3. They are cost effective for the volume and quality of data
4. Are less expensive than conducting 8 to 12 in depth interviews
5. Are time efficient
6. Clients can gain insights by observing the group interaction through a one way mirror.

CHALLENGES

1. Participants can influence each other.
2. Data is not quantifiable.
3. Responses are limited.
4. Data may be difficult to analyze
5. The participants are out of the context of their usual environments.

WHEN TO USE THIS METHOD

1. Know Context
2. Know User
3. Frame insights
4. Explore Concepts

HOW TO USE THIS METHOD

1. Focus groups often take one and a half to two hours.
2. Ask 5 to 10 questions.
3. Define purpose
4. Ask:
   ◦ Why a focus group?
   ◦ Who are the stakeholders?
   ◦ Who is the target population?
   ◦ What problems will be explored?
5. Define resources
6. Write question guide.
7. Recruit participants.
8. Conduct focus group.
9. Analyze data.
10. Create insights.
11. Take actions.

RESOURCES

1. Focus group space.
2. Sound and video recording equipment
3. White board
4. Pens
5. Post-it-notes

REFERENCES

1. Nachmais, Chava Frankfort; Nachmais, David. 2008. Research methods in the Social Sciences: Seventh Edition New York, NY: Worth Publishers

focus group: structured

WHAT IS IT?

With a structured focus group each question has a pre determined time for discussion and when this time is reached the moderator moves the group onto the next question for discussion.

WHO INVENTED IT?

Robert K. Merton 1940 Bureau of Applied Social Research.

WHY USE THIS METHOD?

1. A focus group allows an in depth probe.
2. Interaction between participants can uncover broader insights.
3. They are cost effective for the volume and quality of data
4. Are less expensive than conducting 8 to 12 in depth interviews
5. Are time efficient
6. Clients can gain insights by observing the group interaction through a one way mirror.

CHALLENGES

1. Participants can influence each other.
2. Data is not quantifiable.
3. Responses are limited.
4. Data may be difficult to analyze
5. The participants are out of the context of their usual environments.

WHEN TO USE THIS METHOD

1. Know Context
2. Know User
3. Frame insights
4. Explore Concepts

HOW TO USE THIS METHOD

1. Focus groups often take one and a half to two hours.
2. Ask:
   ◦ Why a focus group?
   ◦ Who are the stakeholders?
   ◦ Who is the target population?
   ◦ What problems will be explored?
3. Define resources
4. Write question guide.
5. Recruit participants.
6. Conduct focus group.
7. Analyze data.
8. Create insights.
9. Take actions.

RESOURCES

1. Focus group space.
2. Sound and video recording equipment
3. White board
4. Pens
5. Post-it-notes

REFERENCES

1. Nachmais, Chava Frankfort; Nachmais, David. 2008. Research methods in the Social Sciences: Seventh Edition New York, NY: Worth Publishers

focus group: teleconference

WHAT IS IT?

This method involves conducting a focus group via teleconference. It allows participation at lower cost from diverse geographical locations.

WHY USE THIS METHOD?

1. A focus group allows an in depth probe.
2. Interaction between participants can uncover broader insights.
3. They are cost effective for the volume and quality of data
4. Are less expensive than conducting 8 to 12 in depth interviews
5. Are time efficient
6. Clients can gain insights by observing the group interaction through a one way mirror.

CHALLENGES

1. Participants cannot read each other's body language.
2. Participants can influence each other.
3. Data is not quantifiable.
4. Responses are limited.
5. Data may be difficult to analyze
6. The participants are out of the context of their usual environments.

WHEN TO USE THIS METHOD

1. Know Context
2. Know User
3. Frame insights
4. Explore Concepts

HOW TO USE THIS METHOD

1. Define purpose
2. Ask:
   ◦ Why a focus group?
   ◦ Who are the stakeholders?
   ◦ Who is the target population?
   ◦ What problems will be explored?
3. Define resources
4. Write question guide.
5. Recruit participants.
6. Conduct focus group.
7. Analyze data.
8. Create insights.
9. Take actions.

RESOURCES

1. Focus group space.
2. Sound and video recording equipment
3. White board
4. Pens
5. Post-it-notes

REFERENCES

1. Nachmais, Chava Frankfort; Nachmais, David. 2008. Research methods in the Social Sciences: Seventh Edition New York, NY: Worth Publishers

focus group: two way

WHAT IS IT?
With this method there are two groups of participants. One group watches the other group's responses. The second group will have different discussions and conclusions based on the first group's responses.

WHO INVENTED IT?
Robert K. Merton 1940 Bureau of Applied Social Research.

WHY USE THIS METHOD?
1. A focus group allows an in depth probe.
2. Interaction between participants can uncover broader insights.
3. They are cost effective for the volume and quality of data
4. Are less expensive than conducting 8 to 12 in depth interviews
5. Are time efficient
6. Clients can gain insights by observing the group interaction through a one way mirror.

CHALLENGES
1. Participants can influence each other.
2. Data is not quantifiable.
3. Responses are limited.
4. Data may be difficult to analyze
5. The participants are out of the context of their usual environments.

WHEN TO USE THIS METHOD
1. Know Context
2. Know User
3. Frame insights
4. Explore Concepts

HOW TO USE THIS METHOD
1. Focus groups often take one and a half to two hours.
2. Ask 5 to 10 questions.
3. Define purpose
4. Ask:
   ◦ Why a focus group?
   ◦ Who are the stakeholders?
   ◦ Who is the target population?
   ◦ What problems will be explored?
5. Define resources
6. Write question guide.
7. Recruit participants.
8. Conduct focus group.
9. Analyze data.
10. Create insights.
11. Take actions.

RESOURCES
1. Focus group space.
2. Sound and video recording equipment
3. White board
4. Pens
5. Post-it-notes

REFERENCES
1. Nachmais, Chava Frankfort; Nachmais, David. 2008. Research methods in the Social Sciences: Seventh Edition New York, NY: Worth Publishers

focus group: unstructured

WHAT IS IT?

An unstructured focus group has flexible moderation. The moderator allows conversations to go in different directions and may allow more time for discussion if required to explore topics.

WHO INVENTED IT?

Robert K. Merton 1940 Bureau of Applied Social Research.

WHY USE THIS METHOD?

1. A focus group allows an in depth probe.
2. Interaction between participants can uncover broader insights.
3. They are cost effective for the volume and quality of data
4. Are less expensive than conducting 8 to 12 in depth interviews
5. Are time efficient
6. Clients can gain insights by observing the group interaction through a one way mirror.

CHALLENGES

1. Participants can influence each other.
2. Data is not quantifiable.
3. Responses are limited.
4. Data may be difficult to analyze
5. The participants are out of the context of their usual environments.

WHEN TO USE THIS METHOD

1. Know Context
2. Know User
3. Frame insights
4. Explore Concepts

HOW TO USE THIS METHOD

1. Focus groups often take one and a half to two hours.
2. Ask:
   ◦ Why a focus group?
   ◦ Who are the stakeholders?
   ◦ Who is the target population?
   ◦ What problems will be explored?
3. Define resources
4. Write question guide.
5. Recruit participants.
6. Conduct focus group.
7. Analyze data.
8. Create insights.
9. Take actions.

RESOURCES

1. Focus group space.
2. Sound and video recording equipment
3. White board
4. Pens
5. Post-it-notes

REFERENCES

1. Nachmais, Chava Frankfort; Nachmais, David. 2008. Research methods in the Social Sciences: Seventh Edition New York, NY: Worth Publishers

focus troupe

WHAT IS IT?
The design team and users act out dramatic vignettes following scripts demonstrating a new product, service or experience. The play presents the problems, and expectations of the design. If actors have some experience of the product or service they can use this.

WHO INVENTED IT?
Sato and Salvador 1999

WHY USE THIS METHOD?
1. You are likely to find new possibilities and problems.
2. Generates empathy for users.
3. This method is an experiential design tool. Bodystorming helps design ideation by exploring context.
4. It is fast and inexpensive.
5. It is a form of physical prototyping
6. It is difficult to imagine misuse scenarios

CHALLENGES
1. Works best with a physical prototype of design.
2. Time is required to write scripts.
3. Some team members may find acting a difficult task.

WHEN TO USE THIS METHOD
1. Know Context
2. Know User
3. Frame insights

HOW TO USE THIS METHOD
1. Select team.
2. Define the locations where a design will be used.
3. Go to those locations and observe how people interact. the artifacts in their environment.
4. Develop the prototypes and props that you need to explore an idea. Identify the people, personas and scenarios that may help you with insight into the design directions.
5. Write scripts
6. Bodystorm the scenarios.
7. Record the scenarios with video and analyze them for insights.

RESOURCES
1. Empathy tools
2. A large room
3. White board
4. Video camera

REFERENCES
1. Understanding Your Users: A Practical Guide to User Requirements Methods By Catherine Courage, Kathy Baxter, Catherine Courage

FREE LIST TEMPLATE

Name of List ....

Prepared for ....

Date ....

Number	Name	Category	Use	Status	Checklist
1					
2					
3					
4					
5					
6					
7					
8					
9					
10					

Signature ....

free list

WHAT IS IT?

A free list is a list all words and concepts related to a particular area that is created by a participant. Because free lists are used to understand group culture frequency is important.

WHO INVENTED IT?

Trotter & Schensul 1998

WHY USE THIS METHOD?

1. Uncovers common perceptions meanings and classification systems
2. Low- cost
3. Little training required
4. Good source for baseline data
5. Works with individuals and groups
6. It is simple.
7. Can be used to compare different groups.
8. Can be used with brainstorming.
9. Helps researchers from using appropriate terms.
10. This method can be used when you have limited time with a group.

CHALLENGES

1. Not a stand alone method
2. Danger of making false associations
3. No accepted ways to check reliability of the procedure.

WHEN TO USE THIS METHOD

1. Know Context
2. Know User
3. Frame insights

HOW TO USE THIS METHOD

1. Consider what information would be valuable
2. Decide which domains you would like to define.
3. Formulate the question.
4. Test your question on several people to ensure the wording is coherent and appropriate.
5. Develop a short set of instructions.
6. Ask the free listing question.
7. It may be necessary to probe your informant for a more comprehensive list.
8. Ask informants to clarify items.
9. Collect data from multiple participants
10. Tally items to calculate the response frequency.
11. Combine the data collected through free listing with other methods to enrich your understanding.

RESOURCES

1. Pens
2. Laptop
3. Paper
4. Note pad.

REFERENCES

1. Borgatti, S. (1998). Elicitation Techniques for Cultural Domain Analysis. In Ethnographer's Toolkit, edited by J. Schensul. Newbury Park: Sage.
2. Weller, S.C. & Romney, A.K. (1988). Systematic Data Collection, Thousand Oaks, CA: Sage.

generative research

WHAT IS IT?

Generative research is research where participants make things to help express their ideas. Generative research can include methods from workshops where participants articulate their ideas by creating models using construction kits to diary methods.

WHO INVENTED IT?

Liz Sanders has been a pioneer of some generative methods.

WHY USE THIS METHOD?

1. Insights come from creative play.
2. Non designers can express their ideas creatively using generative tools.

CHALLENGES

1. Interpretation can be subjective.

WHEN TO USE THIS METHOD

1. Know Context
2. Know User
3. Frame insights

SEE ALSO

1. Diary studies
2. Creative toolkits
3. Photo diaries

RESOURCES

1. Construction kits
2. Diaries
3. White board
4. Pens
5. Creative space

REFERENCES

1. Sanders, E.B.-N. (2001) Virtuosos of the experience domain. In Proceedings of the 2001 IDSA Education Conference.

guerilla ethnography

WHAT IS IT?
Guerrilla ethnography is a collection of low cost responsive and flexible creative research methods. Examples include man on the street interviews, rapid iterative prototypes. remote usability testing. and empathy maps.

WHO INVENTED IT?
Jay Conrad Levinson 1984

WHY USE THIS METHOD?
1. Guerrilla methods are fast,
2. Guerrilla methods are less expensive.
3. Provide direction and data rather than opinions and speculation.
4. Uncover how people think and behave.
5. Provides sufficient insight to make more informed design decisions and guide design decisions.

CHALLENGES
1. Sometime the information gathered is more like a compass for design decisions rather than a road map.

WHEN TO USE THIS METHOD
1. Know Context
2. Know User
3. Frame insights

HOW TO USE THIS METHOD
1. Start by defining an activity, context, and time frame to focus on.
2. Create a plan.
3. Recruit from online sources like Facebook, Mechanical Turk, Ethnio, Craigslist, Twitter, or friends and family.
4. Observe real people in real-life situations
5. Capture Data
6. Reflection and Analysis
7. Brainstorming for solutions
8. Develop prototypes of possible solutions
9. Evaluate and refine the prototypes. Test several iterative refinements.
10. Ask for them to show and tell
11. Listen for pain points and seek opportunities.
12. Don't lead the user to the "right" path
13. Allow for exploration and discovery
14. Make simple prototypes of your favored designs.Only build what you need. No more.

RESOURCES
1. Digital camera
2. Notebook
3. Pens
4. Video camera

REFERENCES
1. Holtzblatt, K., Wendell, J.B., & Wood, S. 2005. Rapid Contextual Design: A How-to guide to key techniques for user-centered design. San Francisco: Morgan-Kaufmann.

ASSESSMENT CRITERIA	CONCEPT 1				CONCEPT 2				CONCEPT 3			
	-2	-1	+1	+2	-2	-1	+1	+2	-2	-1	+1	+2
AESTHETICS	■				■							■
COST		■									■	
TIME TO MARKET	■	■							■			
ROI								■				
EASE OF MAINTENANCE		■	■		■							
ENVIRONMENTAL IMPACT	■	■					■				■	
BRAND COMPLIANCE			■		■				■			
DISTRIBUTION	■						■			■		
USABILITY	■	■	■								■	
COMPLIANCE WITH REGULATIONS						■						■
USE OF EXISTING RESOURCES								■			■	

harris profile

WHAT IS IT?

A Harris Profile is a method for evaluating a number of design alternatives. A four-scale scoring method is used

WHO INVENTED IT?

J. S. Harris,1961

WHY USE THIS METHOD?

1. One chosen/selected alternative from a group of alternatives.
2. Overview of the advantages and disadvantages of the selected alternative.
3. More understanding of the problem and criteria.

WHEN TO USE THIS METHOD

1. Define intent
2. Know Context
3. Know User
4. Frame insights

RESOURCES

1. Pen
2. Paper
3. White board
4. Dry erase markers

HOW TO USE THIS METHOD

1. Select criterion for evaluation.
2. Rate each criteria for each product, service or experience. The scale is coded − 2, − 1, + 1, and + 2.
3. Total the scores.

REFERENCES

1. Harris, J.S. (1961) 'New Product Profile Chart', Chemical and Engineering News, Vol. 39, No. 16, pp.110−118.
2. Roozenburg, N.F.M. and Eekels, J. (1995) Product Design: Fundamentals and Methods, Utrecht: Lemma.

hawthorne effect

WHAT IS IT?

The Hawthorne effect is a psychological theory that the behavior of a person or a group of people will change if they know that they are being observed.

WHO INVENTED IT?

First documented by a research team led by Elton Mayo between 1924 and 1932 at the Western Electric Company Hawthorne plant in Cicero, Illinois. The term was first used by Elton Mayo and Fritz Roethlisberger around 1950.

WHY USE THIS METHOD?

1. Researchers should be aware of the effect to obtain valid results.

CHALLENGES

1. Various writers believe that the original observations and conclusions were overstated including Steven Levitt, John A. List, Adair and H. McIlvaine Parsons

WHEN TO USE THIS METHOD

1. Know Context
2. Know User
3. Frame insights

HOW TO USE THIS METHOD

1. If you conduct a taste test of two beverages and tell the participants who makes the beverages before the test it may influence which beverage that the participants say they prefer.
2. It you tell some participants that they are taking an appetite suppressant then they may eat less even if they are not taking an appetite suppressant.

REFERENCES

1. French, John R. P., "Experiments in Field Settings," in Leon Festinger and Daniel Katz(Eds.), Research Methods in the Behavorial Sciences, Dryden Press, 1953, p. 101.
2. Levitt, Steven D. & List, John A. (2011). "Was There Really a Hawthorne Effect at the Hawthorne Plant? An Analysis of the Original Illumination Experiments". American Economic Journal: Applied Economics 3 (1): 224–238.

heuristic evaluation

WHAT IS IT?
Also known as expert evaluation.
A technique used to identify user problems.
Experts judge whether a user interface follows
a list of established usability heuristics

WHO INVENTED IT?
Jacob Nielsen, 1990 Denmark

WHY USE THIS METHOD?
1. Inexpensive and fast.
2. Can be used early in the design process.
3. Fast feedback.
4. Reliable data.
5. Apply this method before testing
   prototypes with users.

CHALLENGES
1. Focuses on problems
2. Use before research subjects are studied
   for further testing.
3. This method will not uncover all problems.

WHEN TO USE THIS METHOD
1. Know Context
2. Know User
3. Frame insights
4. Explore Concepts

HOW TO USE THIS METHOD
1. Establish a panel of experts.
2. Establish an agreed set of evaluative
   criteria.
3. Brief experts and agree on criteria for the
   evaluation.
4. Each expert inspects the interface alone.
5. After the evaluations the individual
   results are aggregated.
6. A report is prepared which identifies
   a prioritized list of problems with the
   interface.
7. Action the findings of evaluation

RESOURCES
1. A panel of experts
2. A list of heuristic criteria for evaluation.

REFERENCES
1. Nielsen, J., and Molich, R. (1990).
   Heuristic evaluation of user interfaces,
   Proc. ACM CHI'90 Conf. (Seattle, WA, 1—5
   April), 249-256
2. Nielsen, J. (1994). Heuristic evaluation. In
   Nielsen, J., and Mack, R.L. (Eds.), Usability
   Inspection Methods, John Wiley & Sons,
   New York, NY

image: © Aniram | Dreamstime.com

historical method

WHAT IS IT?

Compare something today with something in history. Research the development of a product, service or experience.
Some areas of interest for designers are:
1. An understanding of the origin of an idea.
2. Knowledge of the author of an idea.
3. Local differences

WHO INVENTED IT?

Herodotus 5th century BC, was one of the earliest historians.

WHY USE THIS METHOD?

1. A review of history often uncovers insights relevant to a current design project.
2. Good ideas are sometimes forgotten and need to be rediscovered.
3. We want to avoid revisiting old but unsuccessful solutions

CHALLENGES

1. All constructed histories are written with a viewpoint or bias.
2. Choose sources that have no apparent benefit from presenting a biased account of events.

RESOURCES

1. Primary and secondary historical sources
2. Notebook
3. Pens
4. Digital voice recorder
5. Post-it-notes
6.
Photo: photocase.com - bobot

WHEN TO USE THIS METHOD

1. Know Context
2. Know User
3. Frame insights
4. Explore Concepts

HOW TO USE THIS METHOD

1. Define your subject of research.
2. Find out what secondary sources exist.
3. Create a research plan.
4. Create a goal for your research.
5. Make a list of necessary equipment, people, and materials.
6. Define a schedule for the research.
7. Plan tasks deliverable and milestones with dates.
8. Explore primary Sources.
9. Conduct primary source research.
10. Compile a list of citations.
11. Write the history.
12. Archive the data.

REFERENCES

1. Gilbert J. Garraghan, A Guide to Historical Method, Fordham University Press: New York (1946). ISBN 0-8371-7132-6
2. Martha Howell and Walter Prevenier, From Reliable Sources: An Introduction to Historical Methods, Cornell University Press: Ithaca (2001). ISBN 0-8014-8560-6.
3. R. J. Shafer, A Guide to Historical Method, The Dorsey Press: Illinois (1974). ISBN 0-534-10825-3.

innovation diagnostic

WHAT IS IT?

An innovation diagnostic is an evaluation of an organization's innovation capabilities. It reviews practices by stakeholders which may help or hinder innovation. An innovation diagnostic is the first step in preparing an implementing a strategy to create an organizational culture that supports innovation.

WHY USE THIS METHOD?

1. It helps organizations develop sustainable competitive advantage.
2. Helps identify innovation opportunities
3. Helps develop innovation strategy.

WHEN TO USE THIS METHOD

1. Know Context
2. Know User
3. Frame insights
4. Explore Concepts
5. Make Plans

HOW TO USE THIS METHOD

An innovation diagnostic reviews organizational and stakeholder practices using both qualitative and quantitative methods including

1. The design and development process
2. Strategic practices and planning.
3. The ability of an organization to monitor and respond to relevant trends.
4. Technologies
5. Organizational flexibility
6. Ability to innovate repeatedly and consistently

interview methods

WHAT IS IT?
An interview is a conversation where questions are asked to obtain information.

WHY USE THIS METHOD?
Contextual interviews uncover tacit knowledge about people's context that the people may not be consciously aware of. The information gathered can be detailed.

CHALLENGES
1. Keep control
2. Be prepared
3. Be aware of bias
4. Be neutral
5. Select location carefully

RESOURCES
6. Note pad
7. Confidentiality agreement
8. Digital voice recorder
9. Video camera
10. Digital still camera

WHEN TO USE THIS METHOD
1. Know Context
2. Know User
3. Frame insights

HOW TO USE THIS METHOD
1. Contextual inquiry may be structured as 2 hour one on one interviews.
2. The researcher does not usually impose tasks on the user.
3. Go to the user's context. Talk, watch listen and observe.
4. Understand likes and dislikes.
5. Collect stories and insights.
6. See the world from the user's point of view.
7. Take permission to conduct interviews.
8. Do one-on-one interviews.
9. The researcher listens to the user.
10. 2 to 3 researchers conduct an interview.
11. Understand relationship between people, product and context.
12. Document with video, audio and notes.

RESOURCES
1. Computer
2. Notebook
3. Pens
4. Video camera
5. Release forms
6. Interview plan or structure
7. Questions, tasks and discussion items
8. Confidentiality agreement

REFERENCES
1. Kvale, Steinar. Interviews: An Introduction to Qualitative Research Interviewing, Sage Publications, 1996
2. Foddy, William. Constructing Questions for Interviews, Cambridge University Press, 1993

interview: contextual inquiry

WHAT IS IT?

Contextual inquiry involves one-on-one observations and interviews of activities in the context. Contextual inquiry has four guiding principles:
1. Context
2. Partnership with users.
3. Interpretation
4. Focus on particular goals.

WHO INVENTED IT?

Whiteside, Bennet, and Holtzblatt 1988

WHY USE THIS METHOD?

1. Contextual interviews uncover tacit knowledge about people's context.
2. The information gathered can be detailed.
3. The information produced by contextual inquiry is relatively reliable

CHALLENGES

1. End users may not have the answers
2. Contextual inquiry may be difficult to challenge even if it is misleading.

SEE ALSO

1. Questionnaire
2. Interview
3. Affinity diagram
4. Scenario
5. Persona
6. Ethnography
7. Contextual design

WHEN TO USE THIS METHOD

1. Know Context
2. Know User
3. Frame insights

HOW TO USE THIS METHOD

1. Contextual inquiry may be structured as 2 hour one on one interviews.
2. The researcher does not usually impose tasks on the user.
3. Go to the user's context. Talk, watch listen and observe.
4. Understand likes and dislikes.
5. Collect stories and insights.
6. See the world from the user's point of view.
7. Take permission to conduct interviews.
8. Do one-on-one interviews.
9. The researcher listens to the user.
10. 2 to 3 researchers conduct an interview.
11. Understand relationship between people, product and context.
12. Document with video, audio and notes.

REFERENCES

1. Beyer, H. and Holtzblatt, K., Contextual Design: Defining Customer-Centered Systems, Morgan Kaufmann Publishers Inc., San Francisco (1997).
2. Wixon and J. Ramey (Eds.), Field Methods Case Book for Product Design. John Wiley & Sons, Inc., NY, NY, 1996.

Photo: photocase.com – AlexAlex

interview: contextual interviews

WHAT IS IT?

Contextual inquiry is a user-centered research method. A contextual interview is conducted with people in their own environment. Contextual interviews with users can be conducted in environments such as homes, offices, trains, hospitals or factories. People and researchers collaborate to understand the context.

WHO INVENTED IT?

Whiteside, Bennet, and Holtzblatt 1988

WHY USE THIS METHOD?

Contextual interviews uncover tacit knowledge about people's context that the people may not be consciously aware of. The information gathered can be detailed.

CHALLENGES

1. Keep control
2. Be prepared
3. Be aware of bias
4. Be neutral
5. Select location carefully

WHEN TO USE THIS METHOD

1. Know Context
2. Know User
3. Frame insights

HOW TO USE THIS METHOD

Contextual inquiry is often structured as 2 hour one on one interviews. The researcher does not usually impose tasks on the user. The researcher listens to the user. A contextual interview has three phases:.

1. The introduction. The researcher gives information about the length of the interview, content, confidentiality and method of recording.
2. The body of the interview. The researcher investigates the user in context and documents the information gathered.
3. Wrap up. The researcher goes through the data gathered for verification and clarification by the person being interviewed.

RESOURCES

1. Computer
2. Notebook
3. Pens
4. Video camera
5. Release forms
6. Interview plan or structure
7. Questions, tasks and discussion items
8. Confidentiality agreement

REFERENCES

1. Rubin, Herbert and Irene Rubin. Qualitative Interviewing: The Art of Hearing Data. 2nd edition. Thousand Oaks, CA: Sage Publications, 2004. Print.
2. Kvale, Steinar. Interviews: An Introduction to Qualitative Research Interviewing, Sage Publications, 1996

interview: contextual laddering

WHAT IS IT?

Contextual laddering is a one-on-one interviewing technique done in context. Answers are further explored by the researcher to uncover root causes or core values.

WHO INVENTED IT?

Gutman 1982, Olsen and Reynolds 2001.

WHY USE THIS METHOD?

1. Laddering can uncover underlying reasons for particular behaviors.
2. Laddering may uncover information not revealed by other methods.
3. Complement other methods
4. Link features and product attributes with user/customer values

CHALLENGES

1. Analysis of data is sometimes difficult.
2. Requires a skilled interviewer who can keep the participants engaged.
3. Laddering can be an unpleasant experience for participants because of it's repetitive nature.
4. Sometimes information may not be represented hierarchically.

WHEN TO USE THIS METHOD

1. Know Context
2. Know User
3. Frame insights
4. Explore Concepts

HOW TO USE THIS METHOD

1. Interviews typically take 60 to 90 minutes.
2. The introduction. The researcher gives information about the length of the interview, content, confidentiality and method of recording.
3. The body of the interview. The researcher investigates the user in context and documents the information gathered.
4. Ask participants to describe what kinds of features would be useful in or distinguish different products.
5. Ask why.
6. If this answer doesn't describe the root motivation ask why again.
7. Repeat step 3. until you have reached the root motivation.
8. Wrap up. Verification and clarification

RESOURCES

1. Note pad
2. Confidentiality agreement
3. Digital voice recorder
4. Video camera
5. Digital still camera
6. Interview plan or structure
7. Questions, tasks and discussion items

REFERENCES

1. Reynolds TJ, Gutman J (2001) Laddering theory, method, analysis, and interpretation. In: Reynolds TJ et al (eds) Understanding consumer decision making. The means-end approach to marketing and advertising strategy. Lawrence Erlbaum associates, New Jersey, pp 25—62

interview: conversation cards

WHAT IS IT?
Cards used for initiating conversation in a contextual interview and to help subjects explore.

WHO INVENTED IT?
Originator unknown. Google Ngram indicates the term first appeared around 1801 in England for a collection of "Moral and Religious Anecdotes particularly adapted for the entertainment and instruction of young persons, and to support instead of destroying serious conversation"

WHY USE THIS METHOD?
1. Questions are the springboard for conversations.
2. Can be used to initiate sensitive conversations.

CHALLENGES
1. How will data from the cards be used?
2. How will cards be evaluated?
3. How many cards are necessary to be representative?
4. What are potential problems relating card engagement
5. Use one unit of information per question.

WHEN TO USE THIS METHOD
1. Know Context
2. Know User
3. Frame insights

HOW TO USE THIS METHOD
1. Decide on goal for research.
2. Formulate about 10 questions related to topic
3. Create the cards.
4. Recruit the subjects.
5. Undertake pre interview with sample subject to test.
6. Use release form if required.
7. Carry light equipment.
8. Record answers verbatim.
9. Communicate the purpose and length of the interview.
10. Select location. It should not be too noisy or have other distracting influences
11. Work through the cards.
12. Video or record the sessions for later review.
13. Analyze
14. Create Insights

RESOURCES
1. Conversation Cards.
2. Notebook
3. Video Camera
4. Pens
5. Interview plan or structure
6. Questions, tasks and discussion items

REFERENCES
1. Rubin, Herbert and Irene Rubin. Qualitative Interviewing: The Art of Hearing Data. 2nd edition. Thousand Oaks, CA: Sage Publications, 2004. Print.
2. Kvale, Steinar. Interviews: An Introduction to Qualitative Research Interviewing, Sage Publications, 1996

interview: emotion cards

WHAT IS IT?

Emotion cards are a field method of analyzing and quantifying peoples emotional response to a design. The method classifies emotions into sets of emotions which each can be associated with a specific recognizable facial expression.

The emotion card tool consists of sixteen cartoon-like faces, half male and half female, each representing distinct emotions. Each face represents a combination of two emotion dimensions,Pleasure and Arousal. Based on these dimensions, the emotion cards can be divided into four quadrants: Calm-Pleasant, Calm-Unpleasant, Excited-Pleasant, and Excited-Unpleasant.

WHO INVENTED IT?

Bradley 1994
Pieter Desmet 2001

WHY USE THIS METHOD?

1. It is an inexpensive method.
2. The results are easy to analyze.
3. Emotional responses are subtle and difficult to measure.
4. Emotion cards is a cross-cultural tool.
5. Facial emotions are typically universally recognized

CHALLENGES

1. Emotions of male and female faces are interpreted differently.
2. Sometimes users want to mark more than one picture to express a more complex emotional response.

WHEN TO USE THIS METHOD

1. Know Context
2. Know User
3. Frame insights
4. Explore Concepts

HOW TO USE THIS METHOD

1. Decide the goal of the study.
2. Recruit the participants.
3. Brief the participants.
4. When each interaction is complete the researcher asks the participant to select one of a number of cards that shows facial expressions that they associate with the interaction.

RESOURCES

1. Emotion cards
2. Notebook
3. Pens
4. Video camera
5. Release forms
6. Interview plan or structure
7. Questions, tasks and discussion items

REFERENCES

1. Bradley and Lang. Measuring emotion: the Self-Assessment Manikin and the Semantic Differential. Journal of Behavior Therapy and Experimental Psychiatry, 25, 1 (1994).
2. Desmet, P.M.A. Emotion through expression;designing mobile telephones with an emotional fit. Report of Modeling the Evaluation Structure of KANSEI, 3 (2000), 103-110.

interview: e-mail

WHAT IS IT?
With this method an interview is conducted via an e-mail exchange.

WHY USE THIS METHOD?
1. Extended access to people.
2. Background noises are not recorded.
3. Interviewee can answer the questions at his or her own convenience
4. It is not necessary to take notes
5. It is possible to use online translators.
6. Interviewees do not have to identify a convenient time to talk.

CHALLENGES
1. Interviewer may have to wait for answers.
2. Interviewer is disconnected from context.
3. Lack of communication of body language.

WHEN TO USE THIS METHOD
1. Know Context
2. Know User
3. Frame insight

HOW TO USE THIS METHOD
1. Choose a topic
2. Identify a subject.
3. Contact subject and obtain approval.
4. Prepare interview questions.
5. Conduct interview
6. Analyze data.

RESOURCES
1. Computer
2. Internet connection
3. Notebook
4. Pens
5. Interview plan or structure
6. Questions, tasks and discussion items
7. Confidentiality agreement

REFERENCES
1. Foddy, William. Constructing Questions for Interviews, Cambridge University Press, 1993

interview: extreme user

WHAT IS IT?

Interview experienced or inexperienced users of a product or service. in order to discover useful insights that can be applied to the general users.

WHY USE THIS METHOD?

Extreme user's solutions to problems can inspire solutions for general users. Their behavior can be more exaggerated than general users so it is sometimes easier to develop useful insights from these groups.

CHALLENGES

1. Keep control
2. Be prepared
3. Be aware of bias
4. Be neutral
5. Select location carefully

WHEN TO USE THIS METHOD

1. Know Context
2. Know User
3. Frame insights
4. Explore Concepts

HOW TO USE THIS METHOD

1. Do a timeline of your activity and break it into main activities
2. Identify very experienced or very inexperienced users of a product or service in an activity area.
3. Explore their experiences through interview.
4. Discover insights that can inspire design.
5. Refine design based on insights.

RESOURCES

1. Computer
2. Notebook
3. Pens
4. Video camera
5. Release forms
6. Interview plan or structure
7. Questions, tasks and discussion items
8. Confidentiality agreement

REFERENCES

1. Rubin, Herbert and Irene Rubin. Qualitative Interviewing: The Art of Hearing Data. 2nd edition. Thousand Oaks, CA: Sage Publications, 2004. Print.
2. Kvale, Steinar. Interviews: An Introduction to Qualitative Research Interviewing, Sage Publications, 1996
3. Foddy, William. Constructing Questions for Interviews, Cambridge University Press, 1993

Photo: photocase.com – gregpeppers

interview: group

WHAT IS IT?
This method involves interviewing a group of people.

WHY USE THIS METHOD?
People will often give different answers to questions if interviewed on=on=-one and in groups. If resources are available it is useful to interview people in both situations.

CHALLENGES
1. Group interview process is longer than an individual interview

WHEN TO USE THIS METHOD
1. Know Context
2. Know User
3. Frame insight

RESOURCES
1. Computer
2. Notebook
3. Pens
4. Video camera
5. Release forms
6. Interview plan or structure
7. Questions, tasks and discussion items
8. Confidentiality agreement

HOW TO USE THIS METHOD
1. Welcome everyone and introduce yourself
2. Describe the process.
3. Ask everyone to introduce themselves.
4. Conduct a group activity or warming-up exercise.
5. Break the larger group into smaller groups of 4 or 5 people and give them a question to answer. Ask each participant to present their response to the larger group.
6. Allow about 25 minutes.
7. Ask each interviewee to write a summary
8. Collect the summaries.
9. Ask if have any further comments.
10. Thank everyone and explain the next steps.
11. Give them your contact details.

REFERENCES
12. Kvale, Steinar. Interviews: An Introduction to Qualitative Research Interviewing, Sage Publications, 1996
13. Foddy, William. Constructing Questions for Interviews, Cambridge University Press, 1993

interview: guided storytelling

WHAT IS IT?
Guided storytelling is interview technique, where the designer asks a participant to walk you through a scenario of use for a concept. Directed story telling guides participants to describe their experiences and thoughts on a specific topic.

WHO INVENTED IT?
Whiteside, Bennet, and Holtzblatt 1988

WHY USE THIS METHOD?
1. Guided storytelling uncovers tacit knowledge.

CHALLENGES
1. Keep control
2. Be prepared
3. Be aware of bias
4. Be neutral
5. Select location carefully

WHEN TO USE THIS METHOD
1. Know Context
2. Know User
3. Frame insight

RESOURCES
1. Computer
2. Notebook
3. Pens
4. Video camera
5. Release forms
6. Interview plan or structure
7. Questions, tasks and discussion items
8. Confidentiality agreement

HOW TO USE THIS METHOD
1. Contextual inquiry may be structured as 2 hour one on one interviews.
2. The researcher does not usually impose tasks on the user.
3. Go to the user's context. Talk, watch listen and observe.
4. Understand likes and dislikes.
5. Collect stories and insights.
6. See the world from the user's point of view.
7. Take permission to conduct interviews.
8. Do one-on-one interviews.
9. The researcher listens to the user.
10. 2 to 3 researchers conduct an interview.
11. Understand relationship between people, product and context.

REFERENCES
1. Rubin, Herbert and Irene Rubin. Qualitative Interviewing: The Art of Hearing Data. 2nd edition. Thousand Oaks, CA: Sage Publications, 2004. Print.
2. Kvale, Steinar. Interviews: An Introduction to Qualitative Research Interviewing, Sage Publications, 1996
3. Foddy, William. Constructing Questions for Interviews, Cambridge University Press, 1993

interview: man in the street

WHAT IS IT?

Man in the street interviews are impromptu interviews usually recorded on video. They are usually conducted by two people, a researcher and a cameraman.

WHY USE THIS METHOD?

1. Contextual interviews uncover tacit knowledge.
2. The information gathered can be detailed.

CHALLENGES

1. Keep control
2. Be prepared
3. Be aware of bias
4. Be neutral
5. Ask appropriate questions
6. Select location carefully
7. Create a friendly atmosphere, interviewee to feel relaxed.
8. Clearly convey the purpose of the interview.
9. This method results in accidental sampling which may not be representative of larger groups.

WHEN TO USE THIS METHOD

1. Know Context
2. Know User
3. Frame insights

HOW TO USE THIS METHOD

1. Decide on goal for research.
2. Formulate about 10 questions related to topic
3. Use release form if required.
4. Conduct a preliminary interview.
5. Select location. It should not be too noisy or have other distracting influences
6. Approach people, be polite. Say, "Excuse me, I work for [your organization] and I was wondering if you could share your opinion about [your topic]."
7. If someone does not wish to respond, select another subject to interview.
8. Limit your time. Each interview should be no be longer than about 10 minutes.
9. Conduct 6 to 10 interviews

RESOURCES

1. Video camera
2. release forms

REFERENCES

1. Rubin, Herbert and Irene Rubin. Qualitative Interviewing: The Art of Hearing Data. 2nd edition. Thousand Oaks, CA: Sage Publications, 2004. Print.
2. Kvale, Steinar. Interviews: An Introduction to Qualitative Research Interviewing, Sage Publications, 1996
3. Foddy, William. Constructing Questions for Interviews, Cambridge University Press, 1993

interview: naturalistic group

WHAT IS IT?
Naturalistic group interview is an interview method where the participants know each other prior to the interview and so have conversations that are more natural than participants who do not know each other.

WHY USE THIS METHOD?
1. This method has been applied in research in Asia where beliefs are informed by group interaction.
2. Can help gain useful data in cultures where people are less willing to share their feelings.

CHALLENGES
1. Familiarity of participants can lead to groupthink.

WHEN TO USE THIS METHOD
2. Know Context
3. Know User

HOW TO USE THIS METHOD
1. The interview context should support natural conversation.
2. Select participants who have existing social relationships.
3. Group the participants in natural ways so that the conversation is as close as possible to the type of discussion they would have in their everyday life.
4. Groups should be no larger than four people for best results.

RESOURCES
1. Video camera
2. Note pad
3. Pens
4. Use local moderator

REFERENCES
1. Bengtsson, Anders, and Giana M. Eckhardt. "Naturalistic Group Interviewing in China." Qualitative Market Research: An International Journal. 12:1 (2010): 36–44.

interview: one-on-one

WHAT IS IT?

The one-on-one interview is an interview that is between a researcher and one participant in a face-to-face situation.

WHY USE THIS METHOD?

1. The best method for personal information
2. Works well with other methods in obtaining information to inform design.
3. Can be used to exchange ideas or to gather information to inform design

CHALLENGES

1. Keep control
2. Be prepared
3. Be aware of bias
4. Be neutral
5. Select location carefully
6. Record everything
7. Combine one on one interviews with group interviews.

WHEN TO USE THIS METHOD

1. Know Context
2. Know User
3. Frame insights

RESOURCES

4. Notebook
5. Pens
6. Video camera
7. Release forms
8. Interview plan
9. Questions, and tasks

image: © Kuzma | Dreamstime.com

HOW TO USE THIS METHOD

1. May be structured as 2 hour one on one interviews.
2. Select the questions and the subjects carefully.
3. Create interview guide,
4. Conduct a preinterview to refine the guide.
5. The researcher does not usually impose tasks on the user.
6. Go to the user's context. Talk, watch listen and observe.
7. Understand likes and dislikes.
8. Collect stories and insights.
9. See the world from the user's point of view.
10. Take permission to conduct interviews.
11. Understand relationship between person, product and context.
12. Document with video, audio and notes.

REFERENCES

1. Rubin, Herbert and Irene Rubin. Qualitative Interviewing: The Art of Hearing Data. 2nd edition. Thousand Oaks, CA: Sage Publications, 2004. Print.
2. Kvale, Steinar. Interviews: An Introduction to Qualitative Research Interviewing, Sage Publications, 1996
3. Foddy, William. Constructing Questions for Interviews, Cambridge University Press, 1993

interviews: photo elicitation

WHAT IS IT?

Photos are used by a researcher as a focus to discuss the experiences, thoughts and feelings of participants.

WHY USE THIS METHOD?

1. A method sometimes used to interview children.
2. Photos can make staring a conversation with a participant easier.
3. Photos can uncover meaning which is not uncovered in a face to face interview.

CHALLENGES

1. Photos can create ethical questions for the researcher.
2. A researcher may show bias in selecting subject of photos.

RESOURCES

1. Note pad
2. Pens
3. Camera
4. Video camera
5. Digital voice recorder

WHEN TO USE THIS METHOD

1. Know Context
2. Know User

HOW TO USE THIS METHOD

1. Define the context.
2. Select the participants
3. Either researcher or participant may take the photos.
4. Researcher analyses photos and plans the interview process
5. Researcher shows the photos to the participant and discusses their thoughts in relation to the photographs.
6. The interview is analyzed by the researcher.
7. The researcher creates a list of insights.

REFERENCES

1. M. Clark-Ibáñez. Framing the social world with photo-elicitation interviews. American Behavioral Scientist,47(12):1507--1527, 2004.

interview: structured

WHAT IS IT?

In a structured interview the researcher prepares a list of questions, script or an interview guide that they follow during the interview. Most interviews use a structured method.

WHY USE THIS METHOD?

1. A structured interview is often used for for phone interviews.
2. It is easy to analyze the results.
3. Structured interviews are often used by quantitative researchers.

CHALLENGES

1. Respondents may be less likely to discuss sensitive experiences.

WHEN TO USE THIS METHOD

1. Know Context
2. Know User
3. Frame insight

HOW TO USE THIS METHOD

1. The researcher should follow the script exactly.
2. The interviewer is required to show consistency in behavior across all interviews

RESOURCES

1. Computer
2. Notebook
3. Pens
4. Video camera
5. Release forms
6. Interview plan
7. Questions, and tasks
8. Confidentiality agreement

REFERENCES

1. Rubin, Herbert and Irene Rubin. Qualitative Interviewing: The Art of Hearing Data. 2nd edition. Thousand Oaks, CA: Sage Publications, 2004. Print.
2. Kvale, Steinar. Interviews: An Introduction to Qualitative Research Interviewing, Sage Publications, 1996
3. Foddy, William. Constructing Questions for Interviews, Cambridge University Press, 1993

interview: unstructured

WHAT IS IT?
Unstructured interviews are interviews where questions can be modified as needed by the researcher during the interview.

WHY USE THIS METHOD?
1. A useful technique for understanding how a subject may perform under pressure.
2. Unstructured interviews are used in ethnographies and case studies
3. Respondents may be more likely to discuss sensitive experiences.

CHALLENGES
1. Interviewer bias is unavoidable

WHEN TO USE THIS METHOD
1. Know Context
2. Know User
3. Frame insight

HOW TO USE THIS METHOD
1. Researchers need a list of topics to be covered during the interview

RESOURCES
1. Computer
2. Notebook
3. Pens
4. Video camera
5. Release forms
6. Interview plan
7. Questions, and tasks
8. Confidentiality agreement

REFERENCES
1. Rubin, Herbert and Irene Rubin. Qualitative Interviewing: The Art of Hearing Data. 2nd edition. Thousand Oaks, CA: Sage Publications, 2004. Print.
2. Kvale, Steinar. Interviews: An Introduction to Qualitative Research Interviewing, Sage Publications, 1996
3. Foddy, William. Constructing Questions for Interviews, Cambridge University Press, 1993

interview: telephone

WHAT IS IT?
With this method an interview is conducted via telephone.

WHO INVENTED IT?

WHY USE THIS METHOD?
1. Wide geographical access
2. Allows researcher to reach hard to reach people.
3. Allows researcher to access closed locations.
4. Access to dangerous or politically sensitive sites

CHALLENGES
1. Lack of communication of body language.
2. Interviewer is disconnected from context.

WHEN TO USE THIS METHOD
1. Know Context
2. Know User
3. Frame insight

HOW TO USE THIS METHOD
1. Choose a topic
2. Identify a subject.
3. Contact subject and obtain approval.
4. Prepare interview questions.
5. Conduct interview
6. Analyze data.

RESOURCES
7. Computer
8. Notebook
9. Pens

REFERENCES
1. Rubin, Herbert and Irene Rubin. Qualitative Interviewing: The Art of Hearing Data. 2nd edition. Thousand Oaks, CA: Sage Publications, 2004. Print.
2. Kvale, Steinar. Interviews: An Introduction to Qualitative Research Interviewing, Sage Publications, 1996
3. Foddy, William. Constructing Questions for Interviews, Cambridge University Press, 1993

image: Miklav | Dreamstime.com

idiographic approach

WHAT IS IT?

This method is an intense study of a person emphasizing that person's uniqueness. This differs from research that concentrates on common or repeated forms of behavior

WHO INVENTED IT?

Piaget 1953

WHY USE THIS METHOD?

1. May provide a more in depth understanding of an individual.

CHALLENGES

1. Difficult to generalize findings
2. Freud and Paiget created universal theories on the basis of unrepresentative individuals.

WHEN TO USE THIS METHOD

1. Know Context
2. Know User
3. Frame insights

HOW TO USE THIS METHOD

1. Use case studies
2. Use flexible long term procedures.

RESOURCES

1. Video camera
2. Camera
3. Digital voice recorder
4. Note pad
5. Pens

REFERENCES

1. Cone, J. D. (1986). Idiographic, nomothetic, and related perspectives in behavioral assessment. In R. O. Nelson & S. C. Hayes (Eds.): Conceptual foundations of behavioral assessment (pp. 111—128). New York: Guilford.

longitudinal analysis

WHAT IS IT?
Some research requires long term studies. Longitudinal analysis focuses on studying a group of people over a long period of time The study may continue over decades. This method allows insights into a person's long term development. Longitudinal studies allow designers and researchers to distinguish short from long-term phenomena.

WHY USE THIS METHOD?
1. Longitudinal studies allow design researchers to distinguish short from long-term phenomena, such as poverty or aging.
2. Allows researchers to look at changes over tim

CHALLENGES
1. There is the risk of bias due to incomplete follow up,
2. Longitudinal studies are expensive
3. Participants drop out of the study

RESOURCES
1. Note pad
2. Computer
3. Video camera
4. Camera

WHEN TO USE THIS METHOD
1. Know Context
2. Know User
3. Frame insights

HOW TO USE THIS METHOD
Three types of longitudinal studies:
1. Panel Study: Involves sampling diverse individuals.
2. Cohort Study: Involves selecting a group based on factors such as their age or where they live.
3. Retrospective Study: Involves looking at historical records

REFERENCES
1. Carlson, Neil and et al. "Psychology the Science of Behavior", p. 361. Pearson Canada

magic thing

WHAT IS IT?

A Magic Thing is a prop that is a focus for ideas in the context where an proposed device will be used. It can be a material such as wood or hard foam without surface detail. Participants carry a "magic thing" with them as they undertake their activities in context to imagine how a portable device could function.

WHO INVENTED IT?

Jeff Hawkins. Howard 2002. Jeff Hawkins, one of the inventors of the Palm Pilot PDA, carried a small block of wood to help him brainstorm interaction in various environments.

WHY USE THIS METHOD?

1. It is a form of physical prototype that simulates interaction when little information is available.

CHALLENGES

1. The researcher can put some imaginary constraints on the device so that it's technological capabilities are not too far from reality.

WHEN TO USE THIS METHOD

1. Know Context
2. Know User
3. Frame insights
4. Generate Concepts
5. Create Solutions

HOW TO USE THIS METHOD

1. The researcher briefs the participants on a design scenario.
2. The participants are given a prop, their magic thing.
3. The participants are briefed on the technological capabilities of the magic thing.
4. The participants and design team then The participants act out scenarios in context.
5. The role playing is recorded by video or user diaries.
6. The material is analyzed and insights identified.

RESOURCES

1. A magic thing such as a block of wood about the size of a proposed device.
2. Video camera

REFERENCES

Iacucci, G., Mäkelä A., Ranta, M., Mäntylä, M., Visualizing Context, Mobility and Group Interaction: Role Games to Design Product Concepts for Mobile Communication, In: the Proceeding of COOP'2000, Designing Cooperative Systems Conference, 23–26 May 2000, IOS Press, 2000.

method bank

WHAT IS IT?

A Method Bank is a central bank where design methods are documented by an organization's employees and can be accessed and applied by other employees.

WHO INVENTED IT?

1. Lego have compiled a Design Practice and emerging methods bank Microsoft have a methods bank in their Online User Experience best practice intranet.
2. Starbucks have a methods bank in their online workflow management tool

WHY USE THIS METHOD?

1. This approaches helps document tacit knowledge within an organization.

WHEN TO USE THIS METHOD

1. Define intent
2. Know Context
3. Know User
4. Frame insights
5. Explore Concepts
6. Make Plans
7. Deliver Offering

HOW TO USE THIS METHOD

1. Methods are uploaded to the intranet bank.
2. The bank may include descriptions, video, images charts or sketches.

RESOURCES

1. Intranet
2. Camera
3. Video camera
4. Templates
5. Data base.
6. Computers

market segmentation

WHAT IS IT?
A market segment is a group of people with characteristics in common. A market segment is distinct from other segments, it exhibits common needs; it responds similarly to a market stimulus, and it can be reached by a market intervention.

WHO INVENTED IT?
Wendel Smith 1956

WHY USE THIS METHOD?
1. The purpose for segmenting a market is to allow you to focus on people that are "most likely" to use your design.
2. This will help optimize your return on investment.

CHALLENGES
1. Everyone is different.
2. Market segmentation assumes uniformity.
3. Internet based techniques will allow marketing to be done on a customized individual basis.

WHEN TO USE THIS METHOD
1. Know Context
2. Know User
3. Frame insights
4. Generate Concepts
5. Create Solutions

HOW TO USE THIS METHOD
1. Based on what people do
Use and behavior, activities or interests
2. Based on who people are
3. Based on how people think or feel
Attitudes,Needs behaviors and motivations
4. A combination of factors

REFERENCES
1. What is geographic segmentation' Kotler, Philip, and Kevin Lane Keller. Marketing Management. Prentice Hall, 2006. ISBN 978-0-13-145757-7
2. Goldstein, Doug. "What is Customer Segmentation?" Mind of Marketing.net, May 2007. New York, NY.
3. Sheth-Voss, Pieter. Carreras, Ismael. How Informative is Your Segmentation? A simple new metric yields surprising results, Marketing Research, pages 8-13, Winter 2010, American Marketing Association

mobile ethnography

WHAT IS IT?
Widespread use of mobile devices including laptops, tablets and digital cameras smart phone has enabled new ways of undertaking research and connecting with people with people in their everyday context.

WHY USE THIS METHOD?
1. Can be faster and less expensive than non-digital methods.
2. Data collected real time
3. Access to people may be easier
4. People carry digital devices such as smart phones, cameras, laptops and tablets
5. Data can be gathered in context

CHALLENGES
1. Can miss non verbal feedback.
2. Technology may be unreliable
3. Devices may be expensive

WHEN TO USE THIS METHOD
4. Define intent
5. Know Context
6. Know User
7. Frame insights
8. Explore Concepts
9. Make Plans
10. Deliver Offering

HOW TO USE THIS METHOD
There are many different methods which use or access:
1. Audio conferences
2. Web conferences
3. Virtual in depth interviews
4. Virtual Focus groups
5. Mobile diaries

RESOURCES
1. Smart phones,
2. Cameras,
3. Laptops and tablets
4. Mobile software applications

REFERENCES
1. Coover, R. (2004) 'Using Digital Media Tools and Cross-Cultural Research,Analysis and Representation', Visual Studies19(1): 6–25.
2. Dicks, B., B. Mason, A. Coffey and P. Atkinson (2005) Qualitative Research and Hypermedia: Ethnography for the Digital Age. London: SAGE.
3. Kozinets R.V. (2010a), Netnography. Doing Ethnographic Research Online, Sage, London.

mobile diary study

WHAT IS IT?
A mobile diary studies is a method that uses portable devices to capture a person's experiences in context when and where they happen such as their work place or home. Participants can create diary entries from their location on mobile phones or tablets.

WHY USE THIS METHOD?
1. Most people carry a mobile phone.
2. It is a convenient method of recording diary entries.
3. It is easier to collect the data than collecting written diaries.
4. Collection of data happens in real time.
5. Mobile devices have camera, voice and written capability.

CHALLENGES
1. Can miss non verbal feedback.
2. Technology may be unreliable

WHEN TO USE THIS METHOD
1. Know Context
2. Know User
3. Frame insights

HOW TO USE THIS METHOD
1. Define intent
2. Define audience
3. Define context
4. Define technology
5. Automated text messages are sent to participants to prompt an entry.
6. Analyze data

RESOURCES
1. Smart phones,
2. Cameras,
3. Laptops and
4. Tablets

REFERENCES
Coover, R. (2004) 'Using Digital Media Tools and Cross-Cultural Research,Analysis and Representation', Visual Studies19(1): 6—25.
Dicks, B., B. Mason, A. Coffey and P. Atkinson (2005) Qualitative Research and Hypermedia: Ethnography for the Digital Age. London: SAGE.
Kozinets R.V. (2010a), Netnography. Doing Ethnographic Research Online, Sage, London.

image: © Adamr | Dreamstime.com

mystery shopper

WHAT IS IT?
Mystery shopping tool used to collect information about products and services. Mystery shoppers perform tasks including purchasing a product, submitting complaints, and then produce feedback.

Mystery shopping is also known as:
1. Secret Shopping
2. Experience Evaluation
3. Mystery Customers
4. Spotters
5. Digital Customers
6. Evaluations of employee interactions
7. Audits of employee performance
8. Telephone Checks

WHO INVENTED IT?
It was first used around 1953

WHY USE THIS METHOD?
1. Provides information performance
2. Produces actionable insights.
3. Increases employee and customer levels of satisfaction

CHALLENGES
1. Can be expensive, time consuming and not supported by employees.
2. Ethical issues

Image Copyright RTimages, 2013 Used under license from Shutterstock.com

WHEN TO USE THIS METHOD
1. Know Context
2. Know User
3. Frame insights

HOW TO USE THIS METHOD
1. Form objectives
2. Create evaluation form for mystery shopper
3. Recruit mystery shoppers. Can be internal or external personnel.
4. Train mystery shoppers
5. Conduct evaluation.
6. Analyze results.
7. Formulate conclusions and actions needed.
8. Implement Actions.

RESOURCES
1. Evaluation form
2. Video camera
3. Notebook
4. Digital still camera.

REFERENCES
1. Health Care Taps 'Mystery Shoppers' at Wall Street Journal, August 8, 2006
2. C. Erlich, "Mystery Shopping," Competitive Intelligence Magazine 10(2007): 43–44.
3. Ton Van Der Wiele, Martin Hesselink, and Jos Van Iwaarden, "Mystery Shopping: A Tool to Develop Insight into Customer Service Provision," Total Quality Management 16(2005): 529–541.

network map

WHAT IS IT?
This is a method which maps and helps the researcher understand systems or services that involve many stakeholders. The map identifies the stakeholders, their links, influence and goals.

WHO INVENTED IT?
Eva Schiffer 2004 to 2008

WHY USE THIS METHOD?
1. Inexpensive and fast.
2. Connects to existing research tools and methods
3. Makes implicit knowledge explicit
4. Structures complex reality
5. Flexible for use in different contexts.

RESOURCES
1. Large sheets of paper for network map
2. Felt pens for drawing links
3. Adhesive paper as actor cards
4. Flat discs for building Influence-towers
5. Actor figurines

WHEN TO USE THIS METHOD
1. Know Context
2. Know User
3. Frame insights

HOW TO USE THIS METHOD
1. Define problems and goals.
2. Recruit participants
3. Define interview questions
4. Define network links to study
5. Ask participant to go through the process in detail.
6. Make a card with the name and description of each stakeholder. Place the cards on your map.
7. Show links between the stakeholders as lines on the map.
8. Number the links.
9. Create a legend describing each link.
10. Setting up influence towers:
11. Describe the influence of each stakeholder.?
12. Quantify the strength of influence of each stakeholder.
13. Stack discs next to each stakeholder card showing the relative level of influence.
14. Write descriptions of perceived problems next to each stakeholder.

REFERENCES
1. Eva Schiffer http://netmap.wordpress.com/process-net-map

INTERVIEW PROCESS

Question 1: Who is involved?

Ask: "Who is involved in this process?"Write names on actor cards (with different colors of cards for different groups of actors) and distribute on empty Net-Map sheet.

Question 2: How are they linked?

Ask: "Who is linked to whom?" Go through the different kinds of links one by one Draw arrows between actor cards according to interviewee directions. If two actors exchange something draw double headed arrows. If actors exchange more than one thing, add differently colored arrow heads to existing links.

Question 3: How influential are they?

Ask: "How strongly can actors influence (our complex issue)?" Explain / agree on a definition of influence with your interviewee, clarify that this is about influence only and not influence in the world at large. Ask interviewee to assign influence towers to actors: The higher the influence on the issue at stake, the higher the tower. Towers of different actors can be of the same height. Actors with no influence can be put on ground level. Towers can be as high as participants want. Place influence towers next to actor cards. Verbalize set-up and give interviewee the chance to adjust towers before noting height of tower on the Net-Map.

Question 4: What are their goals?

Ask according to pre-defined goals, actor by actor, e.g. "Does this actor support environmental, developmental goals or both?" Note abbreviations for goals next to actor cards, allow for multiple goals where appropriate, by noting more than one goal next to the actor.

Discussion

Discuss the result with your interview partners. Depending on the goal of this specific mapping process, you might ask your participants to think strategically about the network and develop ideas to improve the situation in the future.

Source: Eva Schiffer http://netmap.wordpress.com/process-net-map

nomothetic approach

WHAT IS IT?

Nomothetic approach is the approach of investigating a large group of people to find general laws of behavior that apply to everybody. The term "nomothetic" comes from the Greek word "nomos" meaning "law"

WHO INVENTED IT?

Wilhelm Windelband (1848—1915), M.T. Conner 1986, R.P.J. Freeman 1993 and O. Sharpe 2005

WHY USE THIS METHOD?

1. Useful for designing mass produced products or services.

CHALLENGES

1. Individuals are unique.
2. Superficial understanding of any single person.

WHEN TO USE THIS METHOD

1. Define intent
2. Know Context
3. Know User
4. Frame insights

REFERENCES

1. Butterworth-Heinemann, Elsevior (2005). Research Methods. British Library: Elsevior Ltd. pp. 32.
2. Cone, J. D. (1986). Idiographic, nomothetic, and related perspectives in behavioral assessment. In R. O. Nelson & S. C. Hayes (Eds.): Conceptual foundations of behavioral assessment (pp. 111—128). New York: Guilford.
3. Thomae, H. (1999). The nomothetic-idiographic issue: Some roots and recent trends. International Journal of Group Tensions, 28(1), 187—215.

object stimulation

WHAT IS IT?

Object stimulation is an idea-generation technique that stimulates different perspectives and ideas.

WHO INVENTED IT?

Clark & Sugrue, 1988

WHY USE THIS METHOD?

1. "According to Gar eld et al. [1997], McFadzean [1996], and Nagasundaram and Bostrom [1993], groups utilizing paradigm-stretching and paradigm-breaking techniques produce more creative ideas "

Source: Elspeth McFadzean

CHALLENGES

1. This technique requires imagination

RESOURCES

1. White board or flip chart
2. Dry erase markers
3. Paper
4. Pens
5. Video camera

REFERENCES

1. McFanzean, E. (1998) The creativity continuum toward a classification of creative problem solving techniques, Creativity and Innovation Management, Vol. 7, No 3, pp. 131–139

WHEN TO USE THIS METHOD

1. Explore Concepts

HOW TO USE THIS METHOD

1. "Write the problem statement on a flip chart.
2. Ask the group members to list objects that are completely unrelated to the problem.
3. Ask one individual to select an object and describe it in detail. The group should use this descriptions a stimulus to generate new and novel ideas.
4. Write each idea on a flip chart.
5. Continue the process until each group member has described an object or until all the objects have been described.
6. Ask the participants to relate the ideas back to the problem and to develop them into practical solutions."

Source: Elspeth McFadzean

observation

WHAT IS IT?

This method involves observing people in their natural activities and usual context such as work environment. With direct observation the researcher is present and indirect observation the activities may be recorded by means such as video or digital voice recording.

WHY USE THIS METHOD?

1. Allows the observer to view what users actually do in context.
2. Indirect observation uncovers activity that may have previously gone unnoticed

CHALLENGES

1. Observation does not explain the cause of behavior.
2. Obtrusive observation may cause participants to alter their behavior.
3. Analysis can be time consuming.
4. Observer bias can cause the researcher to look only where they think they will see useful information.

WHEN TO USE THIS METHOD

1. Know Context
2. Know User
3. Frame insights

HOW TO USE THIS METHOD

1. Define objectives
2. Define participants and obtain their cooperation.
3. Define The context of the observation: time and place.
4. In some countries the law requires that you obtain written consent to video people.
5. Define the method of observation and the method of recording information. Common methods are taking written notes, video or audio recording.
6. Run a test session.
7. Hypothesize an explanation for the phenomenon
8. Predict a logical consequence of the hypothesis
9. Test your hypothesis by observation
10. Analyze the data gathered and create a list of insights derived from the observations.

RESOURCES

1. Note pad
2. Pens
3. Camera
4. Video camera
5. Digital voice recorder

REFERENCES

1. Kosso, Peter (2011). A Summary of Scientific Method. Springer. pp. 9. ISBN 9400716133.

observation: covert

WHAT IS IT?

Covert observation is to observe people without them knowing. The identity of the researcher and the purpose of the research are hidden from the people being observed.

WHY USE THIS METHOD?

1. This method may be used to reduce the effect of the observer's presence on the behavior of the subjects.
2. To capture behavior as it happens.
3. Researcher is more likely to observe natural behavior

CHALLENGES

1. The method raises serious ethical questions.
2. Observation does not explain the cause of behavior.
3. Can be difficult to gain access and maintain cover
4. Analysis can be time consuming.
5. Observer bias can cause the researcher to look only where they think they will see useful information.

RESOURCES

1. Camera
2. Video Camera
3. Digital voice recorder

WHEN TO USE THIS METHOD

1. Know Context
2. Know User

HOW TO USE THIS METHOD

1. Define objectives.
2. Define participants and obtain their cooperation.
3. Define The context of the observation: time and place.
4. In some countries the law requires that you obtain written consent to video people.
5. Define the method of observation and the method of recording information. Common methods are taking written notes, video or audio recording.
6. Run a test session.
7. Hypothesize an explanation for the phenomenon.
8. Predict a logical consequence of the hypothesis.
9. Test your hypothesis by observation
10. Analyze the data gathered and create a list of insights derived from the observations.

REFERENCES

1. Ethical Challenges in Participant Observation: A Reflection on Ethnographic Fieldwork By Li, Jun Academic journal article from The Qualitative Report, Vol. 13, No. 1

observation: direct

WHAT IS IT?
Direct Observation is a method in which a researcher observes and records behavior events, activities or tasks while something is happening recording observations as they are made.

WHO INVENTED IT?
Radcliff-Brown 1910
Bronisław Malinowski 1922
Margaret Mead 1928

WHY USE THIS METHOD?
1. To capture behavior as it happens.

CHALLENGES
1. Observation does not explain the cause of behavior.
2. Analysis can be time consuming.
3. Observer bias can cause the researcher to look only where they think they will see useful information.
4. Obtain a proper sample for generalization.
5. Observe average workers during average conditions.
6. The participant may change their behavior because they are being watched.

RESOURCES
1. Note pad
2. Pens
3. Camera
4. Video Camera
5. Digital voice recorder

WHEN TO USE THIS METHOD
6. Know Context
7. Know User

HOW TO USE THIS METHOD
1. Define objectives.
2. Make direct observation plan
3. Define participants and obtain their cooperation.
4. Define The context of the observation: time and place.
5. In some countries the law requires that you obtain written consent to video people.
6. Define the method of observation and the method of recording information. Common methods are taking written notes, video or audio recording.
7. Run a test session.
8. Hypothesize an explanation for the phenomenon.
9. Predict a logical consequence of the hypothesis.
10. Test your hypothesis by observation
11. Analyze the data gathered and create a list of insights derived from the observations.

REFERENCES
1.   Zechmeister, John J. Shaughnessy, Eugene B. Zechmeister, Jeanne S. (2009). Research methods in psychology (8th ed. ed.). Boston [etc.]: McGraw-Hill. ISBN 9780071283519.

observation: indirect

WHAT IS IT?

This is a method where the observer is unobtrusive and is sometimes used for sensitive research subjects.

WHY USE THIS METHOD?

1. To capture behavior as it happens in it's natural setting.
2. Indirect observation uncovers activity that may have previously gone unnoticed
3. May be inexpensive
4. Can collect a wide range of data

CHALLENGES

1. Observation does not explain the cause of behavior.
2. Analysis can be time consuming.
3. Observer bias can cause the researcher to look only where they think they will see useful information.
4. Obtain a proper sample for generalization.
5. Observe average workers during average conditions.
6. The participant may change their behavior because they are being watched.

WHEN TO USE THIS METHOD

1. Know Context
2. Know User

HOW TO USE THIS METHOD

3. Determine research goals.

RESOURCES

1. Note pad
2. Pens
3. Camera
4. Video Camera
5. Digital voice recorder

REFERENCES

1. Friedman, M. P., & Wilson, R. W. (1975). Application of unobtrusive measures to the study of textbook usage by college students. Journal of Applied Psychology, 60, 659 – 662.
2. Zechmeister, John J. Shaughnessy, Eugene B. Zechmeister, Jeanne S. (2009). Research methods in psychology (8th ed. ed.). Boston [etc.]: McGraw-Hill. ISBN 9780071283519.

observation: non participant

WHAT IS IT?
The observer does not become part of the situation being observed or intervene in the behavior of the subjects. Used when a researcher wants the participants to behave normally. Usually this type of observation occurs in places where people normally work or live

WHY USE THIS METHOD?
1. To capture behavior as it happens.

CHALLENGES
1. Observation does not explain the cause of behavior.
2. Analysis can be time consuming.
3. Observer bias can cause the researcher to look only where they think they will see useful information.
4. Obtain a proper sample for generalization.
5. Observe average workers during average conditions.
6. The participant may change their behavior because they are being watched.

WHEN TO USE THIS METHOD
1. Know Context
2. Know User

HOW TO USE THIS METHOD
1. Determine research goals.
2. Select a research context
3. The site should allow clear observation and be accessible.
4. Select participants
5. Seek permission.
6. Gain access
7. Gather research data.
8. Analyze data
9. Find common themes
10. Create insights

RESOURCES
1. Note pad
2. Pens
3. Camera
4. Video Camera
5. Digital voice recorder

REFERENCES
1. Zechmeister, John J. Shaughnessy, Eugene B. Zechmeister, Jeanne S. (2009). Research methods in psychology (8th ed. ed.). Boston [etc.]: McGraw-Hill. ISBN 9780071283519.

observation: participant

WHAT IS IT?
Participant observation is an observation method where the researcher participates. The researcher becomes part of the situation being studied. The researcher may live or work in the context of the participant and may become an accepted member of the participant's community. This method was used extensively by the pioneers of field research.

WHO INVENTED IT?
Radcliff-Brown 1910
Bronisław Malinowski 1922
Margaret Mead 1928

WHY USE THIS METHOD?
1. The goal of this method is to become close and familiar with the behavior of the participants.
2. To capture behavior as it happens.

CHALLENGES
1. My be time consuming
2. May be costly
3. The researcher may influence the behavior of the participants.
4. The participants may not show the same behavior if the observer was not present.
5. May be language barriers
6. May be cultural barriers
7. May be risks for the researcher.
8. Be open to possibilities.
9. Be sensitive to privacy, and confidentiality.

WHEN TO USE THIS METHOD
1. Know Context
2. Know User

HOW TO USE THIS METHOD
1. Determine research goals.
2. Select a research context
3. The site should allow clear observation and be accessible.
4. Select participants
5. Seek permission.
6. Gain access
7. Gather research data.
8. Analyze data
9. Find common themes
10. Create insights

RESOURCES
1. Note pad
2. Pens
3. Camera
4. Video Camera
5. Digital voice recorder

REFERENCES
1. Malinowski, Bronisław (1929) The sexual life of savages in north-western Melanesia: an ethnographic account of courtship, marriage and family life among the natives of the Trobriand Islands, British New Guinea. New York: Halcyon House.
2. Marek M. Kaminski. 2004. Games Prisoners Play. Princeton University Press. ISBN 0-691-11721-7

observation: overt

WHAT IS IT?
A method of observation where the subjects are aware that they are being observed

WHO INVENTED IT?
Radcliff-Brown 1910
Bronisław Malinowski 1922
Margaret Mead 1928

WHY USE THIS METHOD?
1. To capture behavior as it happens.

CHALLENGES
1. Observation does not explain the cause of behavior.
2. Analysis can be time consuming.
3. Observer bias can cause the researcher to look only where they think they will see useful information.

RESOURCES
1. Note pad
2. Pens
3. Camera
4. Video Camera
5. Digital voice recorder

REFERENCES
1. Zechmeister, John J. Shaughnessy, Eugene B. Zechmeister, Jeanne S. (2009). Research methods in psychology (8th ed. ed.). Boston [etc.]: McGraw-Hill. ISBN 9780071283519.

WHEN TO USE THIS METHOD
1. Know Context
2. Know User

HOW TO USE THIS METHOD
1. Define objectives.
2. Define participants and obtain their cooperation.
3. Define The context of the observation: time and place.
4. In some countries the law requires that you obtain written consent to video people.
5. Define the method of observation and the method of recording information. Common methods are taking written notes, video or audio recording.
6. Run a test session.
7. Hypothesize an explanation for the phenomenon.
8. Predict a logical consequence of the hypothesis.
9. Test your hypothesis by observation
10. Analyze the data gathered and create a list of insights derived from the observations.

observation: structured

WHAT IS IT?
Particular types of behavior are observed and counted like a survey. The observer may create an event so that the behavior can be more easily studied. This approach is systematically planned and executed.

WHY USE THIS METHOD?
1. Allows stronger generalizations than unstructured observation.
2. May allow an observer to study behavior that may be difficult to study in unstructured observation.
3. To capture behavior as it happens.
4. A procedure is used which can be replicated.

CHALLENGES
1. Observation does not explain the cause of behavior.
2. Analysis can be time consuming.
3. Observer bias can cause the researcher to look only where they think they will see useful information.

RESOURCES
1. Note pad
2. Pens
3. Camera
4. Video Camera
5. Digital voice recorder

WHEN TO USE THIS METHOD
1. Know Context
2. Know User

HOW TO USE THIS METHOD
1. Define objectives.
2. Define participants and obtain their cooperation.
3. Define The context of the observation: time and place.
4. In some countries the law requires that you obtain written consent to video people.
5. Define the method of observation and the method of recording information. Common methods are taking written notes, video or audio recording.
6. Run a test session.
7. Hypothesize an explanation for the phenomenon.
8. Predict a logical consequence of the hypothesis.
9. Test your hypothesis by observation
10. Analyze the data gathered and create a list of insights derived from the observations.

REFERENCES
1. Zechmeister, John J. Shaughnessy, Eugene B. Zechmeister, Jeanne S. (2009). Research methods in psychology (8th ed. ed.). Boston [etc.]: McGraw-Hill. ISBN 9780071283519.

observation: unstructured

WHAT IS IT?

This method is used when a researcher wants to see what is naturally occurring without predetermined ideas. We use have an open-ended approach to observation and record all that we observe

WHY USE THIS METHOD?

1. To capture behavior as it happens.
2. This form of observation is appropriate when the problem has yet to be formulated precisely and flexibility is needed in observation to identify key components of the problem and to develop hypotheses
3. Observation is the most direct measure of behavior

CHALLENGES

1. Replication may be difficult.
2. Observation does not explain the cause of behavior.
3. Analysis can be time consuming.
4. Observer bias can cause the researcher to look only where they think they will see useful information.
5. Data cannot be quantified
6. In this form of observation there is a higher probability of observer's bias.

WHEN TO USE THIS METHOD

1. Know Context
2. Know User

HOW TO USE THIS METHOD

1. Select a context to explore
2. Take a camera, note pad and pen
3. Record things and questions that you find interesting
4. Record ideas as you form them
5. Do not reach conclusions.
6. Ask people questions and try to understand the meaning in their replies.

RESOURCES

1. Note pad
2. Pens
3. Camera
4. Video Camera
5. Digital voice recorder

REFERENCES

1. Zechmeister, John J. Shaughnessy, Eugene B. Zechmeister, Jeanne S. (2009). Research methods in psychology (8th ed. ed.). Boston [etc.]: McGraw-Hill. ISBN 9780071283519.

online methods

WHAT IS IT?
Online testing is a method of obtaining feedback for a design relatively quickly and cost effectively. It is an emerging area of design research.
Some areas are:
1. Online ethnography
2. Online focus groups
3. Online interviews
4. Online questionnaires
5. Web-based experiments
6. Online clinical trials

WHY USE THIS METHOD?
1. You can reach a large number of people
2. Flexible
3. Time and cost effective
4. New media seem to offer the hope of reaching different populations of research subjects in new ways
5. Access to populations
6. May be more acceptable method for participants.

CHALLENGES
1. May not be the fastest method of getting feedback.
2. Participants may lose interest quickly.
3. High drop out rates.
4. Participant's input from senses is limited to vision
5. Is a method that is still being adopted.
6. Sensitivity is required in internet research for legal, practical and ethical reasons.

WHEN TO USE THIS METHOD
1. Know Context
2. Know User

HOW TO USE THIS METHOD
This is a complex and growing area of research. Some guidelines are
1. E-mail can be used for online focus groups using the copy all function.
2. Because participants can reply at any time moderation may be more difficult than a face to face focus group.
3. Group interaction may be less than in a face to face interview or focus group.
4. Social networks can be useful in generating lively discussions and allowing interaction within the social context of a group

RESOURCES
1. Computer
2. Text editor
3. Internet connection
4. Social network connections

REFERENCES
1. Fischer, M., Lyon, S. and Zeitlyn, D. (2008) The internet and the future of social science research. In Fielding, N., Lee, R. M. and Blank, G. (Eds.), The SAGE handbook of Online Research Methods. London. SAGE. pp. 519-536.
2. Hewson, C., Yule, P., Laurent, D. and Vogel, C. (2003) Internet Research Methods. London. Sage.

online methods: ethnography

WHAT IS IT?

Online ethnography refers to a number of related online research methods that adapt ethnographic methods to the study of the communities and cultures created through computer-mediated social interaction

WHO INVENTED IT?

One of the early published articles identifying emerging online ethnography was by Arnould and Wallendorf 1994

WHY USE THIS METHOD?

1. New level of access to people
2. Access to more people
3. Easier access than traditional ethnography
4. Less expensive Than traditional ethnography.
5. Faster than traditional methods

CHALLENGES

1. Some believe that new methods need to be developed that are distinctively different than face to face ethnographic methods.

WHEN TO USE THIS METHOD

1. Know Context
2. Know User

HOW TO USE THIS METHOD

There are diverse methods developing for ethnographic study via the internet.

1. Netnography
2. Online Interviews
3. Online focus groups
4. Online Communities and Cultures

RESOURCES

1. Computer
2. Web browser
3. Internet connection

REFERENCES

1. Wilson, Samuel M.; Peterson, Leighton C. (2002). "The Anthropology of Online Communities". Annual Review of Anthropology 31: 449–467.
2. Domínguez, Daniel; Beaulieu, Anne; Estalella, Adolfo; Gómez, Edgar; Schnettler, Bernt & Read, Rosie (2007). Virtual Ethnography. Forum Qualitative Sozialforschung / Forum: Qualitative Social Research, 8(3), http://nbn-resolving.de/urn:nbn:de:0114-fqs0703E19.

online methods: clinical trials

WHAT IS IT?

An online clinical trail involves the use of the internet to conduct a clinical trial in part or in whole.

US National Cancer Institute and the University of California, San Francisco, School of Medicine maintain websites with suggested methods and templates for phase I — III studies. Because of the complexity and critical nature of this method the author suggests that you review those site for more information. [2] [3]

WHO INVENTED IT?

In 2011, the US FDA approved a Phase 1 trial that used remote patient monitoring, to collect data in patients' homes and transmit it electronically to the trial database.

WHY USE THIS METHOD?

1. Using Internet resources may reduce the expense and development time of a clinical trial.
2. The processes of patient registration, randomization, data collection, analysis, and publication can all be accomplished with online resources

CHALLENGES

1. Security is a central issue when considering the Internet for sensitive information exchange

WHEN TO USE THIS METHOD

1. Know Context
2. Know User

REFERENCES

1. The Internet and Clinical Trials: Background, Online Resources, Examples and Issues. James Paul; Rachael Seib; Todd Prescott. Journal of Medical Internet Research Vol 7 (1) 2005
2. US National Cancer Institute, Cancer Therapy Evaluation Program, authors. Protocol templates, applications and guidelines. 2004. [2004 Aug 16]. http://ctep.cancer.gov/guidelines/templates.html.
3. University of California, San Francisco, School of Medicine, authors. UCSF clinical research manuals and guidelines. 2004. [2004 Aug 16]. http://medschool.ucsf.edu/research_forms/

online methods: focus groups

WHAT IS IT?
An online focus group is a focus group conducted via the internet. It is one of a number of online research methods.

WHO INVENTED IT?
Greenfield Online, Inc. Filed a patent on January 22, 1999 for 'System and Method For Conducting Focus Groups Using Remotely Located Participants Over A Computer Network.'

WHY USE THIS METHOD?
1. Consumer research
2. Political research
3. Business to business research.
4. Less expensive and faster to organize than face to face focus groups.
5. Avoids travel expenses.
6. Greater geographic reach.

CHALLENGES
1. Body language less readable

WHEN TO USE THIS METHOD
1. Know Context
2. Know User

HOW TO USE THIS METHOD
1. Invite pre screened qualified subjects who represent the target to participate.
2. Define incentives
3. Prepare questions.
4. Usually usually limited to 8-10 participants.
5. Durations is generally one hour to 90 minutes
6. Can record via web cams participants face while they undertake exercises.
7. Use software that facilitates White board style exercises that are visible to participants.
8. Respondents should interact with each other and with the moderator.

RESOURCES
1. Online focus group interface
2. Computer
3. Web browser
4. Internet connection.

online methods: interviews

WHAT IS IT?
With this method an interview is conducted via internet.

WHY USE THIS METHOD?
1. Possible to access a geographically dispersed population;
2. Possible savings in costs to the researcher
3. Reduce issues of interviewer effect as participants cannot 'see' each other

CHALLENGES
1. Lack of communication of body language.
2. Establishing a good rapport may be more difficult.
3. Higher drop out rate.
4. Lack of visibility of distractions.

RESOURCES
1. Computer
2. Internet connection
3. Notebook
4. Pens
5. Interview plan or structure
6. Questions, tasks and discussion items
7. Confidentiality agreement

WHEN TO USE THIS METHOD
1. Know Context
2. Know User

HOW TO USE THIS METHOD
Technologies include news groups and forums and e-mail.
1. Choose a topic
2. Identify a subject.
3. Contact subject and obtain approval.
4. An asynchronous online interview is one where the researcher and the researched are not necessarily online at the same time.
5. Prepare interview questions.
6. Conduct interview
7. Analyze data.

REFERENCES
1. Mann and Stewart (2005) Internet Communication and Qualitative Research: A Handbook for Researching Online London: Sage

226

online methods: questionnaires

WHAT IS IT?

An online questionnaire is a questionnaire conducted via the internet.

WHY USE THIS METHOD?

1. Web surveys are faster, simpler and cheaper
2. Data collection period is significantly shortened
3. Simple to compile data
4. Complex skip patterns can be implemented in ways that are mostly invisible to the respondent
5. According to ESOMAR online survey research accounted for 20% of global data-collection expenditure in 2006.

CHALLENGES

1. Response rates are generally low
2. Sample selection bias that is out of research control

REFERENCES

1. Burns, A. C., & Bush, R. F. (2010). Marketing Research. Upper Saddle River, NJ: Pearson Education.
2. Foddy, W. H. (1994). Constructing questions for interviews and questionnaires: Theory and practice in social research (New ed.). Cambridge, UK: Cambridge University Press.

WHEN TO USE THIS METHOD

1. Know Context
2. Know User

HOW TO USE THIS METHOD

1. It is recommended that the time taken to complete an online questionnaire should not exceed 5 minutes.
2. Pretest the questionnaire with at least 5 people, prior to publication on the web.
3. The questionnaire should begin with a short introduction that explains to the participant why it is being conducted and what the information will be used for.
4. Use "smart branching" to lessen complexity. Jump to the next relevant question based on a particular answer.
5. Include a "Thank you" statement at the end.
6. Use statements which are interpreted in the same way by different cultures.
7. Use statements where people that have different opinions will give different answers.
8. Use positive statements and avoid negatives or double negatives.
9. Do not make assumptions about the respondent.
10. Use clear and comprehensible wording, easily understandable for all educational levels
11. Avoid items that contain more than one question per item

online methods: experiments

WHAT IS IT?
A internet based experiment is an experiment that is conducted over the Internet.

WHO INVENTED IT?
Early study by Reips and Bosnjak, 2001

WHY USE THIS METHOD?
1. Researchers can collect large amounts of research material from a wide range of locations and people at relatively low expense.

CHALLENGES
1. Web-based experiments may have weaker experimental controls

WHEN TO USE THIS METHOD
1. Know Context
2. Know User

HOW TO USE THIS METHOD
1. Consider using a web-based software tool
2. Pretest your experiment for clarity of instructions and availability on different platforms.
3. Check your Web experiment for configuration errors
4. Run your experiment both online and offline,for comparison.
5. Ask filter questions
6. Check for obvious naming of files,conditions,and,if applicable,passwords.
7. Perform consistency checks.
8. Report and analyze dropout curves

Source [1]

online methods: online ethics

HOW TO USE THIS METHOD
Below are some guidelines for online research.

1. Participant should not be obliged to answer questions
2. Incentives to take a survey should be used as little as possible.
3. Questionnaires should allow respondents to remain anonymous.
4. Sensitive questionnaires should be confidential.
5. Questions should have the option of "I don't know" or an option that denotes neutrality
6. Questions should not trick the participant.
7. Participant should know why the questionnaire is taking place
8. Participant should know what the information will be used for.
9. In sensitive cases, the questionnaire should be reviewed by an ethics committee or outside party.

REFERENCES

1. Reips, Ulf-Dietrich . (2007). The methodology of Internet-based experiments. In A. Joinson, K. McKenna, T. Postmes, & U.-D. Reips (Eds.), The Oxford Handbook of Internet Psychology (pp. 373-390). Oxford: Oxford University Press.
1. Reips Ulf-Dietrich Standards for Internet-Based Experimenting Experimental and Developmental Psychology, 2002 University of Zürich, Switzerland
2. Reips, U.-D. (2002). Standards for Internet-based experimenting. Experimental Psychology, 49 (4), 243-256.

open card sort

WHAT IS IT?
This is a method for discovering the relationships of a list of items. Participants asked to arrange individual, unsorted items into groups. For an open card sort the user defines the groups rather than the researcher.

Card sorting is applied when:
1. When there is a large number of items.
2. The items are similar and difficult to organize into categories.
3. Users may have different perceptions related to organizing the items.

WHO INVENTED IT?
Jastrow 1886
Nielsen & Sano 1995

WHY USE THIS METHOD?
1. It is a simple method using index cards,
2. Used to provide insights for interface design.

CHALLENGES
1. Ask participants to fill ot a second card if they feel it belongs in two groups.
2. There are a number of online card sorting tools available.

RESOURCES
1. Post cards
2. Pens
3. Post-it-notes
4. Laptop computer
5. A table

Image Copyright forest_strider, 2013
Used under license from Shutterstock.com

WHEN TO USE THIS METHOD
1. Know Context
2. Know User
3. Frame insights
4. Explore Concepts

HOW TO USE THIS METHOD
1. Recruit between 5 and 15 participants representative of your user group.
2. Provide a small deck of cards.
3. Provide clear instructions. Ask your participants to arrange the cards in ways that make sense to them. 100 cards takes about 1 hour to sort.
4. The user sorts labelled cards into groups by that they define themselves.
5. The user can generate more card labels.
6. If users do not understand a card ask them to exclude it. Ask participants for their rationale for any dual placements of cards.
7. Analyze the piles of cards and create a list of insights derived from the card sort.
8. Analyze the data. Proximity or similarity matrixes, dendrograms, and tree diagrams help create a taxonomical hierarchy for the items being grouped

REFERENCES
1. Jakob Nielsen (May 1995). "Card Sorting to Discover the Users' Model of the Information Space".
2. Jakob Nielsen (July 19, 2004). "Card Sorting: How Many Users to Test"

open ended questions

WHAT IS IT?

Open ended questions are questions that encourage a broad meaningful responses from a respondent rather than a simple yes or no answer.

WHY USE THIS METHOD?

1. Are more objective than close ended questions
2. Better than close ended questions when probing sensitive topics with respondents.
3. Good method in focus groups.

CHALLENGES

1. Should be combined with close ended questions.
2. Perceived as less threatening than open close ended questions.
3. Take more time than close ended questions

WHEN TO USE THIS METHOD

1. Know Context
2. Know User

HOW TO USE THIS METHOD

1. Ask close ended question first if respondents are not comfortable talking.
2. Follow-up with "Why?" or "How?"
3. Ask questions that encourage people to talk.
4. An example of an open ended question may be "Why did it happen?" or "What happened then?"
5. Try to listen to the answer

RESOURCES

1. Pen
2. Paper
3. Video camera
4. Digital voice recorder
5. Question guide

REFERENCES

1. Howard Schuman and Stanley Presser (October 1979). "The Open and Closed Question". American Sociological Review 44 (5): 692—712.

personal inventory

WHAT IS IT?
This method involves studying the contents of a research subject's purse, or wallet. Study the things that they carry everyday.

WHO INVENTED IT?
Rachel Strickland and Doreen Nelson 1998

WHY USE THIS METHOD?
1. To provide insights into the user's lifestyle, activities, perceptions, and values.
2. to understand the needs priorities and interests

WHEN TO USE THIS METHOD
1. Know Context
2. Know User
3. Frame insights

HOW TO USE THIS METHOD
1. Formulate aims of research
2. Recruit participants carefully.
3. "the participant is asked to bring their 'most often carried bag' and lay the objects they carry on a flat surface, talking through the purpose and last-use of each item. Things to look out for where the bag is kept in the home and what is clustered around it, what is packed/repacked on arrival/departure, and the use of different bags for different activities." *Jan Chipchase*
4. Document the contents with photographs and notes
5. ask your research subject to talk about the objects and their meaning.
6. Analyze the data.

RESOURCES
1. Camera
2. Note pad

PERSONA

PERSONA NAME
....

DEMOGRAPHICS
....
....
....
....

CHARACTERISTIC STATEMENT
....
....
....
....
....

GOALS
....
....
....
....

AMBITIONS
....
....
....
....

INFLUENCERS AND ACTIVITIES
....
....
....
....

SCENARIOS
....
....
....
....

OTHER CHARACTERISTICS

TYPE: ....   TYPE: ....   TYPE: ....   TYPE: ....   TYPE: ....   TYPE: ....   TYPE: ....   TYPE: ....   TYPE: ....

personas

WHAT IS IT?

"A persona is a archetypal character that is meant to represent a group of users in a role who share common goals, attitudes and behaviors when interacting with a particular product or service Personas are user models that are presented as specific individual humans. They are not actual people, but are synthesized directly from observations of real people."(Cooper)

WHO INVENTED IT?

Alan Cooper 1998

WHY USE THIS METHOD?

1. Helps create empathy for users and reduces self reference.
2. Use as tool to analyze and gain insight into users.
3. Help in gaining buy-in from stake holders.

CHALLENGES

1. Portigal (2008) has claimed that personas give a "cloak of smug customer-centricity" while actually distancing a team from engagement with real users and their needs

REFERENCES

1. Pruitt, John & Adlin, Tamara. The Persona Lifecycle : Keeping People in Mind Throughout Product Design. Morgan Kaufmann, 2006. ISBN 0-12-566251-3

WHEN TO USE THIS METHOD

1. Know Context
2. Know User
3. Frame insights
4. Explore Concept

HOW TO USE THIS METHOD

1. Inaccurate personas can lead to a false understandings of the end users. Personas need to be created using data from real users.
2. Collect data through observation, interviews, ethnography.
3. Segment the users or customers
4. Create the Personas
5. Avoid Stereotypes
6. Each persona should be different. Avoid fringe characteristics. Personas should each have three to four life goals which are personal aspirations,
7. Personas are given a name, and photograph.
8. Design personas can be followed by building customer journeys

RESOURCES

1. Raw data on users from interviews or other research
2. Images of people similar to segmented customers.
3. Computer
4. Graphics software

picture cards

WHAT IS IT?

Picture cards is a method that involves using a collection of cards with images and words that help people talk about their life experiences

WHY USE THIS METHOD?

1. Helps people discuss their experiences and feelings relevant to the research topic.
2. It is relatively inexpensive and fast.
3. The cards may make staring in depth conversations easier.

WHEN TO USE THIS METHOD

4. Know Context
5. Know User
6. Frame insights

HOW TO USE THIS METHOD

1. 100 to 150 cards are created with images and words relevant to the research topic.
2. Prepare question guide
3. In the participant session the researcher asks the participant to recall a story about an experience to start a conversation.
4. Include cards that help the participant discuss issues relevant to proposed design.
5. Can video the session with permission.
6. Analyze the data

RESOURCES

1. Deck of picture cards
2. Video camera
3. Note pad

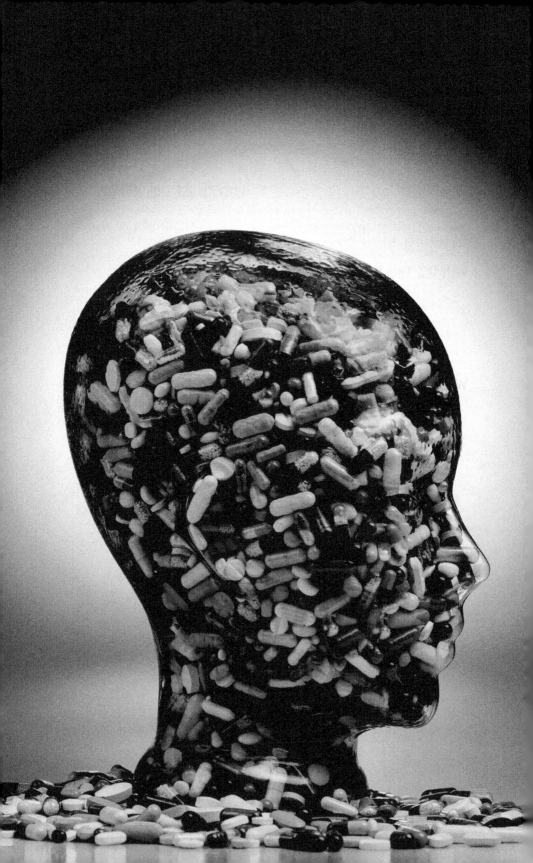

placebo controlled study

WHAT IS IT?
A Placebo-controlled study is a study where a group of subjects receives a treatment and a second group receives a similar treatment that is designed to have no effect.

WHO INVENTED IT?
James Lind 1747

WHY USE THIS METHOD?
1. The purpose of this method is to understand the effects of treatment that do not depend on the treatment itself.

CHALLENGES
1. Ethical questions regarding disclosure
2. Ethical questions regarding the relationship of research and treatment.

WHEN TO USE THIS METHOD
1. Know Context
2. Know User
3. Frame insights

HOW TO USE THIS METHOD
Three groups of participants are created:
1. The group for active treatment
2. The group to receive placebo treatment
3. The group to receive no treatment.

The treatment and placebo treatment are given
The outcomes are observed and compared

REFERENCES
1. Harman WW, McKim RH, Mogar RE, Fadiman J, Stolaroff MJ (August 1966). "Psychedelic agents in creative problem-solving: a pilot study". Psychol Rep 19 (1): 211—27. PMID 5942087.
2. Lasagna L, Mosteller F, von Felsinger JM, Beecher HK (June 1954). "A study of the placebo response". Am. J. Med. 16 (6): 770—9. doi:10.1016/0002-9343(54)90441-6. PMID 13158365.

CRITERIA	CONCEPT 1	CONCEPT 2	CONCEPT 3	CONCEPT 4
Functionality	S	-	-	+
Cost	+	+	+	+
Aesthetics	-	S	-	+
Manufacturability	-	+	+	-
Usability	+	+	-	S
Safety	-	-	-	-
Reliability	-	S	-	-
Maintenance	+	-	-	S
Efficiency	+	+	S	+
Environmental Impact	-	+	-	-
Speed to market	S	-	+	-
Fit with Brand	+	+	-	-
TOTAL	0	2	-3	-2

pugh's matrix

WHAT IS IT?
Pugh's Method is a design evaluation method that uses criteria in an evaluation matrix to compare alternative design directions.

WHO INVENTED IT?
Stuart Pugh 1977

WHY USE THIS METHOD?
1. Overcome shortcomings of design
2. Find different ideas to satisfy criteria
3. Explore alternatives
4. This method can make subjective observations more objective.

CHALLENGES
1. Groupthink
2. Not enough good ideas
3. Taking turns
4. Freeloading
5. Inhibition
6. Lack of critical thinking
7. A group that is too large competes for attention.

WHEN TO USE THIS METHOD
1. Know Context
2. Know User
3. Frame insights
4. Explore Concepts
5. Make Plans

HOW TO USE THIS METHOD
1. Develop the evaluation criteria
2. Identify design criteria to be compared.
3. Design concepts: original design
4. Concepts brainstormed
5. Evaluation matrix: each design evaluated against a best design datum
6. Generate Scores.
7. Calculate the total score
8. Iterate, refine, optimize design
9. Document results

EVALUATION SCALE
+ means substantially better
- means clearly worse
S means more or less the same

RESOURCES
1. White board
2. Dry-erase markers
3. Pens
4. Paper
5. Design Team, 4 to 12 cross disciplinary members
6. Room with privacy

REFERENCES
1. Stuart Pugh, Don Clausing, Ron Andrade, (April 24, 1996). Creating Innovative Products Using Total Design. Addison Wesley Longman. ISBN 0-201-63485-6
2. S. Pugh (1981) Concept selection: a method that works. In: Hubka, V. (ed.), Review of design methodology. Proceedings interna¬tional conference on engineering design, March 1981, Rome. Zürich: Heurista, 1981, blz. 497 – 506.

questionnaires

WHAT IS IT?

A questionnaire is a research tool made up of a number of questions. Questionnaires may be designed for statistical analysis. This is a primary research method.

WHY USE THIS METHOD?

1. Easy to analyze
2. Large sample at relatively low cost.
3. Simple to manage
4. Familiar format
5. Quick to complete
6. Can be used for sensitive topics
7. Respondents have flexibility in time to complete.

WHO INVENTED IT?

Sir Francis Galton 1800s

WHEN TO USE THIS METHOD

1. Know Context
2. Know User
3. Frame insights

CHALLENGES

1. Avoid complex questions
2. Avoid leading questions
3. Avoid jargon
4. Avoid bias
5. Have standard procedure
6. Ask one information at a time
7. Be as simple as possible
8. Adjust the style of the questions to the target audience

HOW TO USE THIS METHOD

1. Define the questions to research
2. Select the participants
3. Prepare the questions
4. Use closed questions with multiple predefined choices or open questions to allow respondents to respond in their own words.
5. Two common closed formats are: the Likert 7 point format: strongly agree, agree, undecided, disagree, strongly disagree. Or 4 point Forced choice format, Strongly agree, agree, disagree, strongly disagree.
6. Pretest the questionnaire
7. Refine the questionnaire
8. Questions should flow logically

REFERENCES

1. Gillham, B. (2008). Developing a questionnaire (2nd ed.). London, UK: Continuum International Publishing Group Ltd
2. Oppenheim, A. N. (2000). Questionnaire design, interviewing and attitude measurement (New ed.). London, UK: Continuum International Publishing Group Ltd

remote evaluation

WHAT IS IT?

Remote evaluation is any usability testing method where the researcher and participant are not in the same location. Remote evaluation may be moderated, or unmoderated.

WHO INVENTED IT?

First published Hartson Castillo Kelson and Neale 1996

WHY USE THIS METHOD?

1. Captures rich feedback
2. Users are in own context
3. Can use for single or multiple participants.
4. May be less expensive and faster.
5. Good for Geographically dispersed user groups.
6. The participant records the data.
7. Face to face evaluation can be expensive, It may be difficult to access participants. and requires a dedicated space.

CHALLENGES

1. You can read body language with in person testing.
2. Difficult to build relationship with participants.
3. Difficult to ensure security of information.
4. Technology can present problems.

WHEN TO USE THIS METHOD

1. Know Context
2. Know User
3. Frame insights

HOW TO USE THIS METHOD

1. Define focus of study.
2. Recruit participants.
3. Typically 5 to 5 participants are used in each iteration of testing.
4. Schedule the evaluation.
5. Brief the participants
6. Run a pilot test.
7. Instruct the participants to say what they are thinking and doing doing and why out loud repeatedly.
8. Users undertake the tasks.
9. Participants undertake a short questionnaire.
10. Researcher review the data and analyzes most common participant problems.
11. Designer implements the changes to the the design based on participant feedback.

RESOURCES

1. Computers
2. Research software

REFERENCES

1. Chalil Madathil, Kapil; Joel S. Greenstein (May 2011). "Synchronous remote usability testing: a new approach facilitated by virtual worlds". Proceedings of the 2011 annual conference on Human factors in computing systems. CHI '11: 2225–2234.
2. Dray, Susan; Siegel, David (March 2004). "Remote possibilities?: international usability testing at a distance". Interactions 11 (2): 10–17. doi:10.1145/971258.971264.

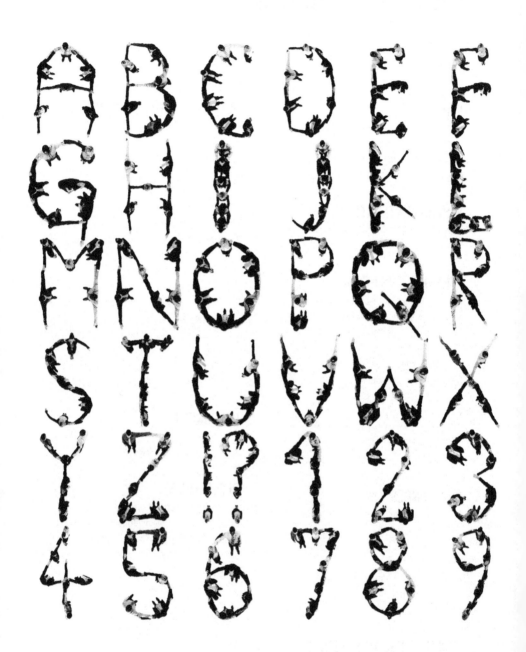

sampling: cluster

WHAT IS IT?

This sampling method is often used to save time and cost when a population is widely dispersed. Dividing a geographic area into clusters is a first step. Following this step, clusters are then sampled.

WHY USE THIS METHOD?

1. May reduce the average cost per interview.

CHALLENGES

1. Higher sampling error than some other methods.

WHEN TO USE THIS METHOD

2. Know Context
3. Know User
4. Frame insights

HOW TO USE THIS METHOD

1. Define the population to be sampled.
2. Divide the population into groups or clusters.
3. Determine the sample size.
4. Select a representative sample from the targeted population.
5. Collect the data from each group.
6. Analyze the data

REFERENCES

1. Kerry and Bland (1998). Statistics notes: The intracluster correlation coefficient in cluster randomisation. British Medical Journal, 316, 1455–1460.
2. Babbie, E. (2001). The Practice of Social Research: 9th Edition. Belmont, CA: Wadsworth Thomson.

sampling: convenience

WHAT IS IT?
A sampling method that uses people who are easily available to sample. Convenience sampling is also known as Opportunity Sampling, Accidental Sampling or Haphazard Sampling.

WHO INVENTED IT?
Pierre Simon Laplace pioneered sampling 1786

WHY USE THIS METHOD?
1. Use when time is limited
2. Use when budgets are limited

CHALLENGES
3. Use as many people as possible.

WHEN TO USE THIS METHOD
1. Know Context
2. Know User

HOW TO USE THIS METHOD
1. Use people in the street, friends, work colleagues, customers, fellow students.

REFERENCES
1. Cochran, William G. (1977). Sampling techniques (Third ed.). Wiley. ISBN 0-471-16240-X
2. Robert Groves, et alia. Survey methodology (2010) Second edition of the (2004) first edition ISBN 0-471-48348-6.
3. Chambers, R L, and Skinner, C J (editors) (2003), Analysis of Survey Data, Wiley, ISBN 0-471-89987-9

sampling: random

WHAT IS IT?

With random also called probability sampling, all people in the population being studied have some opportunity of being included in the sample, and the mathematical probability that any one of them will be selected can be calculated.

WHO INVENTED IT?

Pierre Simon Laplace pioneered sampling 1786

WHY USE THIS METHOD?

1. Applicable when population is small, homogeneous & readily available
2. Each person has an equal probability of selection.
3. Estimates are easy to calculate.

CHALLENGES

1. Minority subgroups of interest in population may not be present in sample in sufficient numbers for study.
2. Requires selection of relevant stratification variables which can be difficult.
3. Is not useful when there are no homogeneous subgroups.
4. Can be expensive to implement.

WHEN TO USE THIS METHOD

1. Know Context
2. Know User

HOW TO USE THIS METHOD

1. Define the population to be sampled.
2. Specifying a sampling frame, a set of items or events possible to measure
3. Determine the sample size.
4. Select a representative sample from the targeted population.
5. Implement the sampling plan. A table of random numbers or lottery system is used to determine which are to be selected.
6. Carefully collect required data.

REFERENCES

1. Cochran, William G. (1977). Sampling techniques (Third ed.). Wiley. ISBN 0-471-16240-X
2. Robert Groves, et alia. Survey methodology (2010) Second edition of the (2004) first edition ISBN 0-471-48348-6.
3. Chambers, R L, and Skinner, C J (editors) (2003), Analysis of Survey Data, Wiley, ISBN 0-471-89987-9

sampling: expert

WHAT IS IT?
A method of sampling where experts with a high level of knowledge are sampled.

WHO INVENTED IT?
Pierre Simon Laplace pioneered sampling 1786

WHY USE THIS METHOD?
1. The opinions of experts are respected.
2. May be credible with audience that accepts the people sampled as experts.

CHALLENGES
1. Not everyone will have the same definition of an expert.

WHEN TO USE THIS METHOD
1. Know Context
2. Know User

HOW TO USE THIS METHOD
1. If a pre study define the definition of an expert for the purpose of the sampling process.
2. Select those people who pass the definition of an expert for the sample.

REFERENCES
1. Cochran, William G. (1977). Sampling techniques (Third ed.). Wiley. ISBN 0-471-16240-X
2. Robert Groves, et alia. Survey methodology (2010) Second edition of the (2004) first edition ISBN 0-471-48348-6.
3. Chambers, R L, and Skinner, C J (editors) (2003), Analysis of Survey Data, Wiley, ISBN 0-471-89987-9

sampling: situation

WHAT IS IT?
Situation sampling involves observation of behavior in different locations, circumstances and conditions.

WHO INVENTED IT?
Pierre Simon Laplace pioneered sampling 1786

WHY USE THIS METHOD?
1. Situation sampling enhances the external validity of findings.
2. By sampling behavior in several different situations, you are able to determine whether the behavior in question changes as a function of the context in which you observed it.
3. Your ability to generalize any behavioral consistencies across the various situations is increased.

WHEN TO USE THIS METHOD
1. Know Context
2. Know User

HOW TO USE THIS METHOD
1. When two individuals observe the same behavior, it is possible to see how well their observations agree.

REFERENCES
1. Cochran, William G. (1977). Sampling techniques (Third ed.). Wiley. ISBN 0-471-16240-X
2. Robert Groves, et alia. Survey methodology (2010) Second edition of the (2004) first edition ISBN 0-471-48348-6.
3. Chambers, R L, and Skinner, C J (editors) (2003), Analysis of Survey Data, Wiley, ISBN 0-471-89987-9

sampling: stratified

WHAT IS IT?
A sampling method that addresses the differences of subgroups, called strata, and ensures that a representative percentage is drawn from each stratum to form the sample.

WHO INVENTED IT?
Pierre Simon Laplace pioneered sampling 1786

WHY USE THIS METHOD?
1. Use when there are specific sub-groups to investigate.
2. May achieve greater statistical significance in a smaller sample.
3. May reduce standard error.

WHEN TO USE THIS METHOD
4. Know Context
5. Know User

HOW TO USE THIS METHOD
1. Divide the population up into a set of smaller non-overlapping sub-groups (strata), then do a simple random sample in each sub-group.
2. Strata can be natural groupings, such as age ranges or ethnic origins.

Source: changingminds.org

REFERENCES
1. Cochran, William G. (1977). Sampling techniques (Third ed.). Wiley. ISBN 0-471-16240-X
2. Robert Groves, et alia. Survey methodology (2010) Second edition of the (2004) first edition ISBN 0-471-48348-6.
3. Chambers, R L, and Skinner, C J (editors) (2003), Analysis of Survey Data, Wiley, ISBN 0-471-89987-9

sampling: systematic

WHAT IS IT?
A variation of random sampling in which members of a population are selected at a predetermined interval from a listing, time period, or space. Systematic sampling is also called systematic random sampling. Use when it is easiest to select every nth person.

WHO INVENTED IT?
Pierre Simon Laplace pioneered sampling 1786

WHY USE THIS METHOD?
1. Use when a stream of representative people are available.
2. Use when it is easiest to select every nth person.
3. Use when it is difficult to identify items using a simple random sampling method.

REFERENCES
1. Cochran, William G. (1977). Sampling techniques (Third ed.). Wiley. ISBN 0-471-16240-X
2. Robert Groves, et alia. Survey methodology (2010) Second edition of the (2004) first edition ISBN 0-471-48348-6.
3. Chambers, R L, and Skinner, C J (editors) (2003), Analysis of Survey Data, Wiley, ISBN 0-471-89987-9

WHEN TO USE THIS METHOD
1. Know Context
2. Know User

HOW TO USE THIS METHOD
1. "Identify your sample size, n. Divide the total number of items in the population, N, by n. Round the decimal down. This gives you your interval, k.
2. Thus for a population of 2000 and a sample of 100, k = 2000/100 = 20.
3. Put the population into a sequential order, ensuring the attribute being studied is randomly distributed.
4. Select a random number, x, between 1 and k.
5. The first sampled item is the x-th. Then select every k-th item.
6. Thus if k is 20 and x is 12, select the 12th item, then the 32nd, then the 52nd and so on.
7. In brief: select every nth item, starting with a random one"

Source: changingminds.org

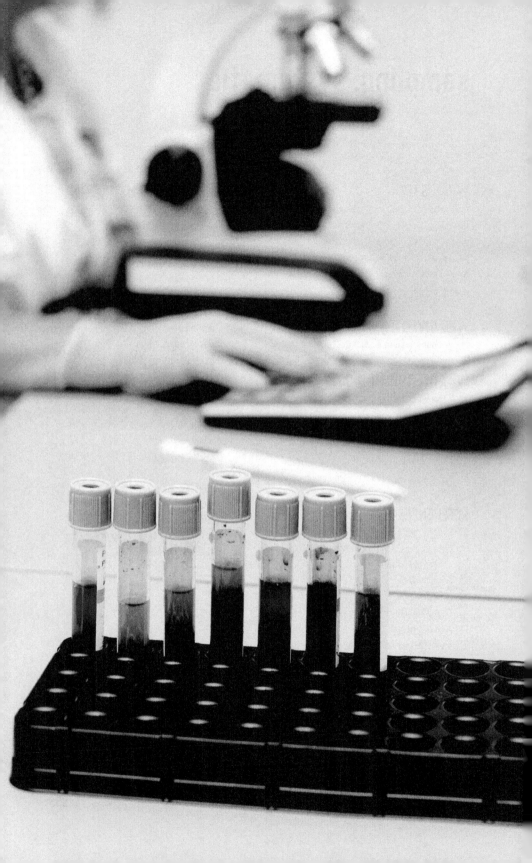

sampling: time

WHAT IS IT?
Researchers choose time intervals for making observations.

WHO INVENTED IT?
Pierre Simon Laplace pioneered sampling 1786

WHY USE THIS METHOD?
The main advantages of sampling are:
1. The cost is lower,
2. Data collection is faster,
3. Time sampling is a useful way to collect and present observation data over a long period of time

CHALLENGES
1. Be careful to record events according to your plan.

WHEN TO USE THIS METHOD
1. Know Context
2. Know User

HOW TO USE THIS METHOD
1. Determine the goal of the research.
2. Select a place and participants.
3. Create a chart to record your data.
4. Carefully collect required data.

REFERENCES
1. Cochran, William G. (1977). Sampling techniques (Third ed.). Wiley. ISBN 0-471-16240-X
2. Robert Groves, et alia. Survey methodology (2010) Second edition of the (2004) first edition ISBN 0-471-48348-6.
3. Chambers, R L, and Skinner, C J (editors) (2003), Analysis of Survey Data, Wiley, ISBN 0-471-89987-9

shadowing

WHAT IS IT?

Shadowing is observing people in context. The researcher accompanies the user and observes user experiences and activities. It allows the researcher and designer to develop design insights through observation and shared experiences with users.

WHO INVENTED IT?

Alex Bavelas 1944
Lucy Vernile, Robert A. Monteiro 1991

WHY USE THIS METHOD?

1. This method can help determine the difference between what subjects say they do and what they really do.
2. It helps in understanding the point of view of people. Successful design results from knowing the users.
3. Define intent
4. Can be used to evaluate concepts.

CHALLENGES

1. Selecting the wrong people to shadow.
2. Hawthorne Effect, The observer can influence the daily activities under being studied.

WHEN TO USE THIS METHOD

1. Know Context
2. Know User
3. Frame insights
4. Generate Concepts

HOW TO USE THIS METHOD

1. Prepare
2. Select carefully who to shadow.
3. Observe people in context by members of your design team.
4. Capture behaviors that relate to product function.
5. Identify issues and user needs.
6. Create design solutions based on observed and experienced user needs.
7. Typical periods can be one day to one week.

RESOURCES

1. Video camera
2. Digital still camera
3. Note pad
4. Laptop Computer

SEE ALSO

1. Day in the life
2. Fly on the wall

REFERENCES

1. McDonald, Seonaidh. "Studying Actions in Context: A Qualitative Shadowing Method for Organizational Research." Qualitative Research. The Robert Gordon University. SAGE Publications. London. 2005. p455–473.
2. Alan Bryman, Emma Bell. Business Research Meythods. Oxford University Press 2007 ISBN 978-0-19-928498-6

image: © Vwimage | Dreamstime.com

SOCIOGRAM

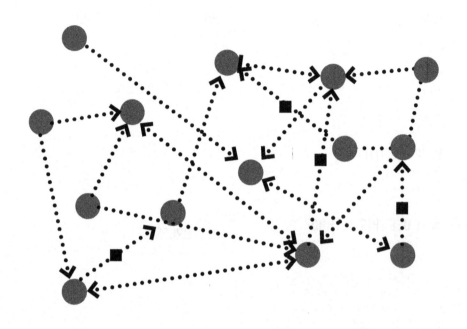

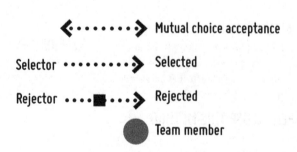

sociogram

WHAT IS IT?

A sociogram is a map of team interactions and structure. It is used to foster partnerships, team cohesiveness and participation.

WHO INVENTED IT?

J. L. Moreno 1934

WHY USE THIS METHOD?

1. A sociogram identifies alliances within the group.

REFERENCES

1. "An Experiential Approach to Organization Development 7th ed."Brown, Donald R.and Harvey, Don. Page 134

WHEN TO USE THIS METHOD

1. Define intent
2. Frame insights
3. Deliver Offering

HOW TO USE THIS METHOD

1. The moderator performs ongoing team observations.
2.   Notes are recorded on team observations
3. A sociogram is drawn and shared with the team.
4. An open discussion follows on ways to improve the team's interactions and performance.
5. The team and moderator develop a strategy for improving team performance and interactions.

RESOURCES

1. Paper
2. Pens
3. White board
4. Dry erase markers

PATIENT STAKEHOLDER MAP

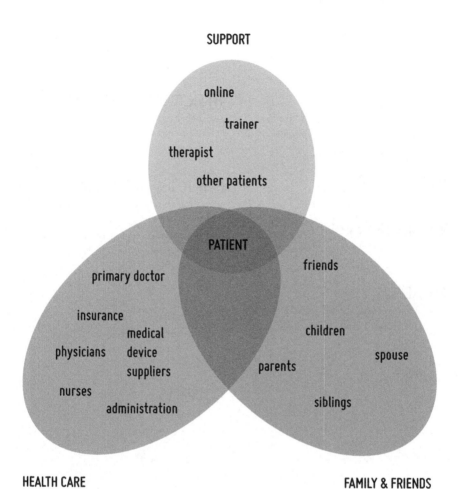

SUPPORT

online

trainer

therapist

other patients

PATIENT

primary doctor

friends

insurance

medical

physicians   device

children

spouse

suppliers

parents

nurses

administration

siblings

HEALTH CARE

FAMILY & FRIENDS

stakeholder map

WHAT IS IT?

Stakeholders maps are used to document the key stake holders and their relationship. They can include end users, those who will benefit, those who may be adversely affected, those who hold power and those who may sabotage design outcomes. At the beginning of a design project it is important to identify the key stake holders and their relationships. The map serves as a reference for the design team.

WHO INVENTED IT?

Mitchell 1997

WHY USE THIS METHOD?

1. Stakeholder mapping helps discover ways to influence other stakeholders.
2. Stakeholder mapping helps discover risks.
3. Stakeholder mapping helps discover positive stakeholders to involve in the design process.

CHALLENGES

1. Stakeholder mapping helps discover negative stakeholders and their associated risks.

RESOURCES

1. White board
2. Post-it-notes
3. Pens
4. Dry-erase markers
5. Interview data

WHEN TO USE THIS METHOD

1. Define intent
2. Know Context
3. Know User
4. Frame insights

HOW TO USE THIS METHOD

1. Develop a categorized list of the members of the stakeholder community.
2. Assign priorities
3. Map the 'highest priority' stakeholders.
4. Can initially be documented on a white board, cards, post-it-notes and consolidated as a diagram through several iterations showing hierarchy and relationships.

Some of the commonly used 'dimensions' include:
1. Power (three levels)
2. Support (three levels)
3. Influence (three levels)
4. Need (three levels)

REFERENCES

1. Mitchell, R. K., B. R. Agle, and D.J. Wood. (1997). "Toward a Theory of Stakeholder Identification and Salience: Defining the Principle of Who and What really Counts." in: Academy of Management Review 22(4): 853 - 888
2. Savage, G. T., T. W. Nix, Whitehead and Blair. (1991). "Strategies for assessing and managing organizational stakeholders." In: Academy of Management Executive 5(2): 61 – 75.

STORYBOARD

PROJECT

NAME

DATE

PAGE

DIALOGUE

ACTION

DIALOGUE

ACTION

DIALOGUE

ACTION

storyboards

WHAT IS IT?

The storyboard is a narrative tool derived from cinema. A storyboard is a form of prototyping which communicates each step of an activity, experience or interaction. Used in films and multimedia as well as product and UX design. Storyboards consists of a number of 'frames' that communicate a sequence of events in context.

WHO INVENTED IT?

Invented by Walt Disney in 1927. Disney credited animator Webb Smith with creating the first storyboard. By 1937–38 all studios were using storyboards.

WHY USE THIS METHOD?

1. Can help gain insightful user feedback.
2. Conveys an experience.
3. Can use a storyboard to communicate a complex task as a series of steps.
4. Allows the proposed activities to be discussed and refined.
5. Storyboards can be used to help designers identify opportunities or use problems.

CHALLENGES

1. Interaction between the storyboard and a user is limited (Landay & Myers, 1996).
2. Participants may not be able to draw well.
3. There haven't been conclusive studies about the effectiveness of storyboards for some design activities.
4. Storyboarding is linear.
5. Not useful for detailed design.

WHEN TO USE THIS METHOD

1. Generate Concepts
2. Create Solutions

HOW TO USE THIS METHOD

1. Decide what story you want to describe.
2. Choose a story and a message: what do you want the storyboard to express?
3. Create your characters
4. Think about the whole story first rather than one panel at a time.
5. Create the drafts and refine them through an iterative process. Refine.
6. Illustrations can be sketches or photographs.
7. Consider: Visual elements, level of detail, text, experiences and emotions, number of frames, and flow of time.
8. Keep text short and informative.
9. 6 to 12 frames.
10. Tell your story efficiently and effectively.
11. Brainstorm your ideas.

RESOURCES

1. Pens
2. Digital camera
3. Storyboard templates
4. Comic books for inspiration

REFERENCES

1. Giuseppe Cristiano Storyboard Design Course: Principles, Practice, and Technique Barron's Educational Series (October 1, 2007) ISBN-10: 0764137328

surveys

WHAT IS IT?

Surveys are a method of collecting information. Surveys collect data usually from a large number of participants. A survey may be undertaken to study objects or animals as well as people. Surveys may take the form of a questionnaire or a face to face interview.

WHO INVENTED IT?

Sir Francis Galton 1800s

WHY USE THIS METHOD?

1. Easy to analyze
2. Large sample at relatively low cost.
3. Simple to manage
4. Familiar format
5. Quick to complete
6. Can be used for sensitive topics
7. Respondents have flexibility in time to complete.

CHALLENGES

1. Avoid complex questions
2. Avoid leading questions
3. Avoid jargon
4. Avoid bias
5. Have standard procedure
6. Ask one information at a time
7. Be as simple as possible
8. Adjust the style of the questions to the target audience

WHEN TO USE THIS METHOD

1. Know Context
2. Know User
3. Frame insights

HOW TO USE THIS METHOD

1. Define topics for research
2. Define the participants
3. Prepare the questions
4. Use closed questions with multiple predefined choices or open questions to allow respondents to respond in their own words.
5. Two common closed formats are: the Likert 7 point format: strongly agree, agree, undecided, disagree, strongly disagree. Or 4 point Forced choice format, Strongly agree, agree, disagree, strongly disagree.
6. Pretest the questionnaire
7. Refine the questionnaire
8. Questions should flow logically

REFERENCES

1. Gillham, B. (2008). Developing a questionnaire (2nd ed.). London, UK: Continuum International Publishing Group Ltd
2. Oppenheim, A. N. (2000). Questionnaire design, interviewing and attitude measurement (New ed.). London, UK: Continuum International Publishing Group Ltd.

BLUEPRINT

ACTIVITY PHASE	CUSTOMER ACTIONS	TOUCHPOINTS	LINE OF INTERACTION	DIRECT CONTACT	LINE OF VISIBILITY	BACK OFFICE	EMOTIONAL EXPERIENCE
							+
							−

swimlanes

WHAT IS IT?

Diagram that shows parallel streams for user, business, and technical process flows. You can include a storyboard lane. Create a blueprint for each persona, interaction or scenario. Provides a focus for discussion and refinement of services or experiences. They may document activities over time such as:

1. Customer Actions
2. Touch points
3. Direct Contact visible to customers
4. Invisible back office actions
5. Support Processes
6. Physical Evidence
7. Emotional Experience for customer.

WHO INVENTED IT?

Lynn Shostack 1983

WHY USE THIS METHOD?

1. Can be used for design or improvement of existing services or experiences.
2. Is more tangible than intuition.
3. Makes the process of service development more efficient.
4. A common point of reference for stakeholders for planning and discussion.
5. Tool to assess the impact of change.

WHEN TO USE THIS METHOD

1. Know Context
2. Know User
3. Frame insights

HOW TO USE THIS METHOD

1. Define the service or experience to focus on.
2. A blueprint can be created in a brainstorming session with stakeholders.
3. Define the customer demographic.
4. See though the customer's eyes.
5. Define the activities and phases of activity under each heading.
6. Link the contact or customer touchpoints to the needed support functions
7. Use post-it-notes on a white board for initial descriptions and rearrange as necessary drawing lines to show the links.
8. Create the blueprint then refine iteratively.

RESOURCES

1. Paper
2. Pens
3. White board
4. Dry-erase markers
5. Camera
6. Blueprint templates
7. Post-it-notes

REFERENCES

1. (1991) G. Hollins, W. Hollins, Total Design: Managing the design process in the service sector, Trans Atlantic Publications
2. (2004) R. Kalakota, M.Robinson, Services Blueprint: Roadmap for Execution, Addison-Wesley, Boston.

talk out loud protocol

WHAT IS IT?
Think aloud or thinking out loud protocols involve participants verbalizing their thoughts while performing a set of tasks. Users are asked to say whatever they are looking at, thinking, doing, and experiencing. A related method is the think-aloud protocol where subjects also explain their actions.

WHO INVENTED IT?
Clayton Lewis IBM 1993

WHY USE THIS METHOD?
1. Provides an understanding of the user's mental model and interaction with the product.
2. Enables observers to see first-hand the process of task completion
3. The terminology the user uses to express an idea or function the design or and documentation.
4. Allows testers to understand how the user approaches the system.

CHALLENGES
1. The design team needs to be composed of people with a variety of skills.

WHEN TO USE THIS METHOD
1. Know Context
2. Know User
3. Frame insights
4. Explore Concepts

HOW TO USE THIS METHOD
1. Identify users.
2. Choose representative tasks.
3. Create a mock-up or prototype.
4. Select participants.
5. Provide the test users with the system or prototype to be tested and tasks.
6. Brief participants.
7. Take notes of everything that users say, without attempting to interpret their actions and words.
8. Iterate
9. Videotape the tests, then analyze the videotapes.

RESOURCES
1. Computer
2. Video camera
3. Note pad
4. Pens

taxonomies

WHAT IS IT?

A taxonomy is a method of organizing groups of items based on their characteristics. It is a way of organizing a large number of ideas or things. Tagging items on the web is a form of taxonomy. Taxonomies are becoming more important as access to information increases. A taxonomy provides a way to describe content.

WHO INVENTED IT?

Taxonomy has been called "the world's oldest profession", One of the earliest recorded was written by Shen Nung, Emperor of China c. 3000 BC. The most widely-known and used taxonomy system is named for the Swedish biologist Carolus Linnaeus.

WHY USE THIS METHOD?

1. A taxonomy is useful to understand the relationships between a group of objects, living organisms or ideas.
2. A taxonomy makes it easier to find an item

WHEN TO USE THIS METHOD

1. Define intent
2. Know Context
3. Know User
4. Frame insights
5. Explore Concepts

HOW TO USE THIS METHOD

1. A taxonomy needs to be relevant to stakeholders.
2. Define the subject of the field or discipline or domain
3. Create tentative list of terms for your taxonomy
4. Organize the information into main categories
5. Identify synonyms
6. Look for gaps
7. Capture the knowledge of users and experts.

RESOURCES

1. Paper
2. Pens
3. White board
4. Dry-erase markers

REFERENCES

1. McGarty, C. (1999). Categorization in Social Psychology, SAGE Publications.
2. Manktelow, M. (2010) History of Taxonomy. Lecture from Dept. of Systematic Biology, Uppsala University. atbi.eu/summerschool/files/ summerschool/Manktelow_Syllabus.pdf
3. McGarty, C. (1999). Categorization in Social Psychology, SAGE Publications.

teachback

WHAT IS IT?

In the teachback method an expert explains a concept to a non-expert.The non-expert then tries to teach back what the expert had explained. During the teachback session, the expert corrects any misunderstandings.

WHY USE THIS METHOD?

1. Teachback is a way to confirm that you have explained what needs to be known in a manner that is understood.
2. The method can highlight concepts that are hard to understand.
3. Everyone benefits from clear information.
4. A chance to check for understanding and, if necessary, re-teach the information.

CHALLENGES

1. The teachback method is not highly structured.
2. It is hard to identify people at risk of misunderstanding.

WHEN TO USE THIS METHOD

1. Know Context
2. Know User
3. Frame insights
4. Deliver Offering

HOW TO USE THIS METHOD

1. Use Plain Language, avoid technical terms, talk slowly, break it down into short statements, focus on the 2 or 3 most important concepts.
2. Ask the subject to repeat in his or her own words how he or she understands the concept explained. If a process was demonstrated to the subject ask the subject to demonstrate it, "I want to be sure I explained everything clearly. Can you please explain it back to me so I can be sure I did?"
3. Ask the subject to verbalize their understanding to ensure that it is correct.
4. Repeat Steps 2 and 3 as necessary.
5. Ask the subject to explain or demonstrate how they will undertake an activity.

REFERENCES

1. Johnson, L. & Johnson, N.E., (1987). Knowledge Elicitation Involving Teachback Interviewing in Kidd, A.L., (Ed.), 1987, Knowledge Acquisition for Expert

through other eyes

WHAT IS IT?

At several times during a design project it is useful to invite an outside group to review the state of the design and to tell your design team if they think that your design direction is real and good.

WHY USE THIS METHOD?

1. A design team can follow design directions that seem unworkable or unrealistic to end users because they may be remote from the end users of a product or service.

WHEN TO USE THIS METHOD

1. Explore concepts

RESOURCES

1. Pen
2. Paper
3. White board
4. Dry erase markers

HOW TO USE THIS METHOD

1. Define your design problem clearly
2. Select a group of outside people who are representative of the end users of a product or service.
3. Prepare a presentation that may include prototypes or images and statements that clearly communicate the favored concept direction.
4. Prepare a question guide to help your design team obtain useful feedback
5. Review your design with the outside group.
6. Refine your design based on the feedback
7. Provide feedback to the outside reviewers to let them know how their input has been useful.
8. It may be necessary to ask the external participants to sign a non disclosure agreement before to the design review.

unfocus group

WHAT IS IT?

Unfocus groups is a qualitative research method in which interviewers hold group interviews where the subjects are selected based on diverse viewpoints and backgrounds The participants may not be users of the product or service.

WHO INVENTED IT?

Uses methods pioneered by Liz Sanders and the consulting firm IDEO circa 2001

WHY USE THIS METHOD?

1. Goal is to get diverse perspectives.

CHALLENGES

1. Participants are removed from their usual context.
2. Non target market group may not be able to effectively define a product or service for target group.

WHEN TO USE THIS METHOD

1. Define intent
2. Know Context
3. Know User
4. Frame insights
5. Explore Concepts
6. Make Plans

HOW TO USE THIS METHOD

1. Assemble a diverse group of participants. Choose Diverse Participants Who:
   ◦ Are not likely to use the product or service,
   ◦ Are highly motivated.
   ◦ Are extreme users of the product
   ◦ Have a tangential connection with the product
   ◦ Don't want the product.
2. Select a good moderator.
3. Prepare a screening questionnaire.
4. Decide incentives for participants.
5. Select facility.
6. Recruit participants.
7. Provide refreshments.
8. Prepare the space. Participants should sit around a large table.
9. Describe rules.
10. First question should encourage talking and participation.
11. Provide simple materials such as paper and ask the participants to create crude prototypes for discussion.
12. Ask participants to act out ideas.
13. Record the feedback for idea generation phase.
14. Follow discussion guide.
15. At end of focus group summarize key points.
16. Moderator collects forms and debriefs focus group.

think out loud protocol

WHAT IS IT?

Think aloud or thinking out loud protocols involve participants verbalizing their thoughts while performing a set of tasks. Users are asked to say whatever they are looking at, thinking, doing, and feeling.

A related but method is the talk-aloud protocol. where participants describe their activities but do not give explanations. This method is thought to be more objective

WHO INVENTED IT?

Clayton Lewis IBM 1993

WHY USE THIS METHOD?

1. Helps a researcher understand interaction with a product or service,.
2. Enables observers to see first-hand the process of task completion
3. The terminology the user uses to express an idea or function the design or and documentation.
4. Allows testers to understand how the user approaches the system.

CHALLENGES

1. The design team needs to be composed of persons with a variety of skills.
2. Pick a diverse, cross disciplinary team.

WHEN TO USE THIS METHOD

1. Know Context
2. Know User
3. Frame insights
4. Explore Concepts

HOW TO USE THIS METHOD

1. Identify users.
2. Choose Representative Tasks.
3. Create a Mock-Up or Prototype.
4. Select Participants.
5. Provide the test users with the system or prototype to be tested and tasks.
6. Brief participants.
7. Take notes of everything that users say, without attempting to interpret their actions and words.
8. Iterate
9. Videotape the tests, then analyze the videotapes.

RESOURCES

1. Computer
2. Video camera
3. Note pad
4. Pens

REFERENCES

1. Lewis, C. H. (1982). Using the "Thinking Aloud" Method In Cognitive Interface Design (Technical report). RC-9265.

triangulation

WHAT IS IT?

Triangulation is a research method where the researcher uses more than two research methods in one study to see if the different methods give similar findings. One example of triangulation is to compare observed behavior with the responses of a survey.

WHO INVENTED IT?

The comes from surveying where triangles are used to create a map.

WHY USE THIS METHOD?

1. Useful when analyzing large data sets.
2. It is employed in quantitative and qualitative research.
3. Helps overcome bias of a single method.
4. It may help the credibility of research conclusions.

CHALLENGES

1. There may be more than one valid conclusion from studying real world people and contexts.

WHEN TO USE THIS METHOD

1. Know Context
2. Know User
3. Frame insights

HOW TO USE THIS METHOD

Types of triangulation approaches include:
1. Dat triangulation where the researcher uses several different strategies for collecting data.
2. Researcher triangulation where more than one researcher is used
3. Method triangulation where more than one method is used to gather data.

REFERENCES

1. Denzin, N. (2006). Sociological Methods: A Sourcebook. Aldine Transaction. ISBN 978-0-202-30840-1. (5th edition).

wizard of oz

WHAT IS IT?
Wizard of Oz method is a research method in which research participants interact with a computer interface that subjects believe to be responding to their input, but which is being operated by an unseen person. The unseen operator is sometimes called the "wizard"

WHO INVENTED IT?
John F. Kelley
Johns Hopkins University. 1980 USA
Nigel Cross

WHY USE THIS METHOD?
1. Wizard of Oz is good for the testing of preliminary interface prototypes.
2. A relatively inexpensive type of simulation
3. Identify problems with an interface concept
4. Investigate visual affordance of an interface.

CHALLENGES
1. Requires training for the wizard.
2. It is difficult for wizards to provide consistent responses across sessions.
3. Computers respond differently than humans
4. It is difficult to evaluate systems with a complex interface using this method.

WHEN TO USE THIS METHOD
1. Know Context
2. Know User
3. Frame insights
4. Explore Concepts

HOW TO USE THIS METHOD
1. The wizard sits in a place not visible to the research participant.
2. The wizard observes the user's actions, and initiates the system's responses.
3. The "wizard" watches live video from a camera focused on the participant's hands and simulate the effects of the participant's actions.
4. Users are unaware that the actions of the system are being produced by the wizard.

RESOURCES
1. Video camera
2. Software interface prototype
3. Computers

REFERENCES
1. Höysniemi, J., Hämäläinen, P., and Turkki, L. 2004. Wizard of Oz prototyping of computer vision based action games for children. In Proceeding of the 2004 Conference on interaction Design and Children: Building A Community (Maryland, June 1–03, 2004). IDC '04. ACM Press, New York, NY, 27-34

Photo: photocase.com – el raph

index

index

index

index

other titles in the
design methods series

Design Methods 1
200 ways to apply design thinking

Author: Robert A Curedale
Published by:
Design Community College Inc.
PO Box 1153
Topanga CA 90290 USA

Edition 1 November 2013

ISBN-10:0988236206
ISBN-13:978-0-9882362-0-2

Design Methods 2
200 more ways to apply design thinking

Author: Robert A Curedale
Published by:
Design Community College Inc.
PO Box 1153
Topanga CA 90290 USA

Edition 1 January 2013

ISBN-13: 978-0988236240
ISBN-10: 0988236249

The Design Thinking Manual

Author: Robert A Curedale
Published by:
Design Community College Inc.
PO Box 1153
Topanga CA 90290 USA

Edition 1 January 2013

ISBN-10: 0988236214
ISBN-13: 978-0-9882362-1-9

50 Brainstorming Methods

Author: Robert A Curedale
Published by:
Design Community College Inc.
PO Box 1153
Topanga CA 90290 USA

Edition 1 January 2013

ISBN-10: 0988236230
ISBN-13: 978-0-9882362-3-3

Structured Workshops

The author presents workshops online and in person in global locations for executives, engineers, designers, technology professionals and anyone interested in learning and applying these proven innovation methods. For information contact: info@curedale.com

about the author

Rob Curedale was born in Australia and worked as a designer, director and educator in leading design offices in London, Sydney, Switzerland, Portugal, Los Angeles, Silicon Valley, Detroit, and China. He designed and managed over 1,000 products and experiences as a consultant and in-house design leader for the world's most respected brands. Rob has three decades experience in every aspect of product development, leading design teams to achieve transformational improvements in operating and financial results. He has extensive experience in forging strategic growth, competitive advantage, and a background in expanding business into emerging markets through user advocacy and extensive cross cultural expertise. Rob's designs can be found in millions of homes and workplaces around the world.

Rob works currently as a Adjunct Professor at Art Center College of Design in Pasadena and consults to organizations in the United States and internationally and presents workshops related to design. He has taught as a member of staff and presented lectures and workshops at many respected design schools and universities throughout the world including Yale, Pepperdine University, Art Center Pasadena, Loyola University, Cranbrook, Pratt, Art Center Europe; a faculty member at SCA and UTS Sydney; as Chair of Product Design and Furniture Design at the College for Creative Studies in Detroit, then the largest product design school in North America, Art Institute Hollywood, Cal State San Jose, Escola De Artes e Design in Oporto Portugal, Instituto De Artes Visuals, Design e Marketing, Lisbon, Southern Yangtze University, Jiao Tong University in Shanghai and Nanjing Arts Institute in China.

Rob's design practice experience includes projects for HP, Philips, GEC, Nokia, Sun, Apple, Canon, Motorola, Nissan, Audi VW, Disney, RTKL, Governments of the UAE,UK, Australia, Steelcase, Hon, Castelli, Hamilton Medical, Zyliss, Belkin, Gensler, Haworth, Honeywell, NEC, Hoover, Packard Bell, Dell, Black & Decker, Coleman and Harmon Kardon. Categories including furniture, healthcare, consumer electronics, sporting, homewares, military, exhibits, packaging. His products and experiences can be found in millions of homes and businesses throughout the world.

Rob established and manages the largest network of designers and architects in the world with more than 300,000 professional members working in every field of design.